A Student Road Map to Better Spelling

Teacher Answer Guide

Book C

Louisa Moats, Ed.D.
and
Bruce Rosow, M.A.

ISBN 1-57035-609-2

Edited by Karen Butler and Sandra L. Knauke
Text layout and design by Sue Campbell and Sherri Rowe
Cover design by Sue Campbell
Production assistance by Eileen Bechtold and Tracy Katzenberger
Illustrated by Tom Zilis

14 13 12 11 10 8 7 6 5 4 3

Printed in the United States of America
Published and Distributed by

Sopris West®
EDUCATIONAL SERVICES

A Cambium Learning® Company

4093 Specialty Place • Longmont, Colorado 80504
(303) 651-2829 • www. sopriswest.com

(25689/03-09)

Contents

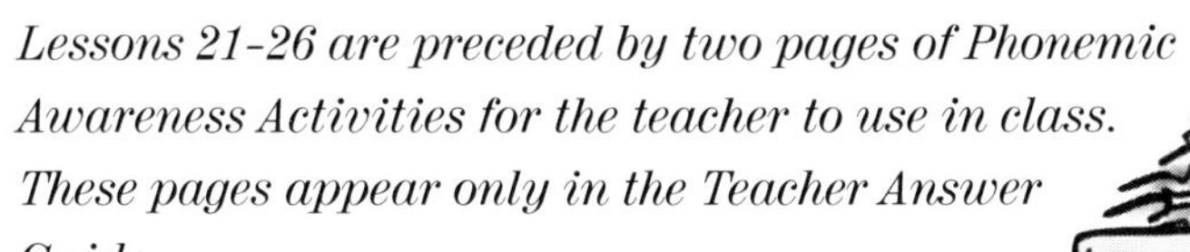

Lessons 21-26 are preceded by two pages of Phonemic Awareness Activities for the teacher to use in class. These pages appear only in the Teacher Answer Guide.

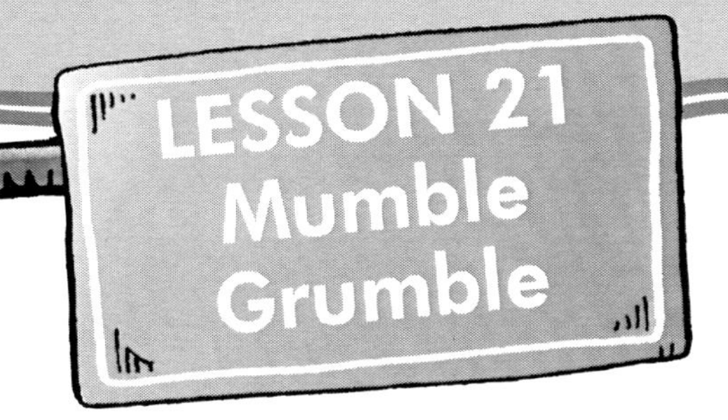

Phonemic Awareness Activities

1. **Segmentation Activity** Hold up the number of fingers—or show the number of markers—that is equal to the number of sounds (phonemes) in each of these words. (Count /əl/ as one sound.)

   a. **Introductory Set** (includes consonant + **-le** syllables)

bun	**bundle**	**am**	**Sam**	**sample**	
/b/ /ŭ/ /n/	/b/ /ŭ/ /n/ /d/ /əl/	/ă/ /m/	/s/ /ă/ /m/	/s/ /ă/ /m/ /p/ /əl/	
ram	**ramble**	**bramble**	**rack**	**crack**	**crackle**
/r/ /ă/ /m/	/r/ /ă/ /m/ /b/ /əl/	/b/ /r/ /ă/ /m/ /b/ /əl/	/r/ /ă/ /k/	/k/ /r/ /ă/ /k/	/k/ /r/ /ă/ /k/ /əl/
rug	**struggle**	**in**	**pin**	**spin**	**spindle**
/r/ /ŭ/ /g/	/s/ /t/ /r/ /ŭ/ /g/ /əl/	/ĭ/ /n/	/p/ /ĭ/ /n/	/s/ /p/ /ĭ/ /n/	/s/ /p/ /ĭ/ /n/ /d/ /əl/
wreck	**freckle**	**rack**	**crack**	**crackle**	
/r/ /ĕ/ /k/	/f/ /r/ /ĕ/ /k/ /əl/	/r/ /ă/ /k/	/k/ /r/ /ă/ /k/	/k/ /r/ /ă/ /k/ /əl/	

   b. vowel + **-r Set**

burp	**purple**	**dirt**	**turtle**	**are**	**mar**	**marble**
/b/ /er/ /p/	/p/ /er/ /p/ /əl/	/d/ /er/ /t/	/t/ /er/ /t/ /əl/	/ar/	/m/ /ar/	/m/ /ar/ /b/ /əl/

art	**tart**	**start**	**startle**	**irk**	**circle**
/ar/ /t/	/t/ /ar/ /t/	/s/ /t/ /ar/ /t/	/s/ /t/ /ar/ /t/ /əl/	/er/ /k/	/s/ /er/ /k/ /əl/

her	**hurt**	**herd**	**hurdle**	**par**	**park**	**spark**	**sparkle**
/h/ /er/	/h/ /er/ /t/	/h/ /er/ /d/	/h/ /er/ /d/ /əl/	/p/ /ar/	/p/ /ar/ /k/	/s/ /p/ /ar/ /k/	/s/ /p/ /ar/ /k/ /əl/

Phonemic Awareness Activities (Continued)

c. **/n/ and /ng/ Set**

an	and	hand	handle	bun	bunk	bungle
/ă/ /n/	/ă/ /n/ /d/	/h/ /ă/ /n/ /d/	/h/ /ă/ /n/ /d/ /əl/	/b/ /ŭ/ /n/	/b/ /ŭ/ /ng/ /k/	/b/ /ŭ/ /ng/ /əl/
fan	**fang**	**angle**	**dangle**	**win**	**wing**	**mingle**
/f/ /ă/ /n/	/f/ /ă/ /ng/	/ă/ /ng/ /əl/	/d/ /ă/ /ng/ /əl/	/w/ /ĭ/ /n/	/w/ /ĭ/ /ng/	/m/ /ĭ/ /ng/ /əl/

d. **Tongue-Flapping Set** (use /D/ to represent the tongue-flapping sound)

bat	battle	cat	cattle	rid	riddle	
/b/ /ă/ /t/	/b/ /ă/ /D/ /əl/	/k/ /ă/ /t/	/k/ /ă/ /D/ /əl/	/r/ /ĭ/ /d/	/r/ /ĭ/ /D/ /əl/	
tie	**title**	**sigh**	**cycle**	**beet**	**beetle**	
/t/ /ī/	/t/ /ī/ /t/ /əl/	/s/ /ī/	/s/ /ī/ /k/ /əl/	/b/ /ē/ /t/	/b/ /ē/ /t/ /əl/	
add	**pad**	**paddle**	**rat**	**rattle**	**lit**	**little**
/ă/ /d/	/p/ /ă/ /d/	/p/ /ă/ /D/ /əl/	/r/ /ă/ /t/	/r/ /ă/ /D/ /əl/	/l/ /ĭ/ /t/	/l/ /ĭ/ /D/ /əl/

2. **Substitution Task** Substitute the first sound with the second sound to make a new word.

riddle /r/ – /f/	**simple** /s/ – /p/	**hurtle** /h/ – /t/	**shingle** /sh/ – /m/
rattle /D/ – /f/	**cattle** /D/ – /k/	**bottle** /D/ – /b/	**riddle** /D/ – /p/

3. **Deletion Task** Say each word after deleting the identified sound (phoneme).

bridle without /əl/	**sparkle** without /əl/	**tackle** without /əl/	**steeple** without /əl/
sprinkle without /sp/	**cripple** without /k/	**title** without second /t/	**fable** without /f/
crumple without /k/	**stable** without /s/	**little** without /əl/	**bobble** without /əl/

Dictate words in the lesson word list for Pretest and Posttest administration. Modify the number of words as needed.

Lesson 21 Word List

1.	wobble	13.	bungle
2.	bugle	14.	peddle
3.	simple	15.	cycle
4.	turtle	16.	beetle
5.	noble	17.	startle
6.	riddle	18.	dwindle
7.	circle	19.	beagle
8.	bridle	20.	brittle
9.	babble	21.	twinkle
10.	little	22.	steeple
11.	sparkle	23.	shingle
12.	title	24.	disable

Spelling Concept: The consonant + **-le** (**c + -le**) syllable.

This week, we are studying a very odd and mystifying new syllable, the consonant + **-le** (**c + -le**) syllable. There are enough things about the **c + -le** syllable to baffle even smart thinkers like Thunker. If you suspect that the Anglo-Saxon language stream—the source of our murkiest spelling oddities—is where this **c + -le** comes from, then you are right. If you also suspect that the evil and devious schwa (ə) is involved, then you are doubly right. This adds up to double trouble!

So let's start with something nice, normal, and even lovable about **c + -le** syllables. It is very easy to know where to divide **c + -le** words into syllables; from the end of the word simply count back three letters, and divide just before the **c + -le** syllable:

ca–**ble**

fum–**ble**

noo–**dle**

mid–**dle**

puz–**zle**

Divide this lesson's study words into syllables. Then, sort your words by the type of *first* syllable among the specific groups.

Closed		Open	Vowel Team	v + -r
wob-ble	ped-dle	bu-gle	bee-tle	tur-tle
sim-ple	dwin-dle	no-ble	bea-gle	cir-cle
rid-dle	brit-tle	bri-dle	stee-ple	spar-kle
bab-ble	twin-kle	ti-tle		star-tle
lit-tle	shin-gle	cy-cle		
bun-gle	dis-a-ble			

a. What are the two types of syllables above that have long vowel sounds?

open vowel team

b. What spelling pattern signals that the vowel in a first syllable will be short?

Two consonants follow a single vowel in a base word.

Lesson 21 Word List

1. wobble	7. circle	13. bungle	19. beagle
2. bugle	8. bridle	14. peddle	20. brittle
3. simple	9. babble	15. cycle	21. twinkle
4. turtle	10. little	16. beetle	22. steeple
5. noble	11. sparkle	17. startle	23. shingle
6. riddle	12. title	18. dwindle	24. disable

Alphabet Soup Write each set of words in alphabetical order.

a b c d e f g h i j k l m n o p q r s t u v w x y z

Set 1:

sparkle shingle
steeple simple startle

1. shingle
2. simple
3. sparkle
4. startle
5. steeple

Set 2:

brittle babble bungle
beagle bugle beetle bridle

1. babble
2. beagle
3. beetle
4. bridle
5. brittle
6. bugle
7. bungle

Spelling Concept: Four aspects of <u>c + -le</u> syllables.

Here, for the first time ever, is Professor Fuzzy Thunker's list of the most baffling and annoying things about <u>c + -le</u> syllables. See if you agree.

Is It or Isn't It? The schwa (ə) vowel rears its ugly self in syllables that aren't accented—that is, where the vowel sound is muffled and muddy. These unaccented vowel sounds are the same sounds you would make if you saw a worm part in your spaghetti and said "/ə/" or "/uh/" (not "EEEK!" It's just a worm, not a pachyderm!). We say that accented syllables play fair, and unaccented syllables sometimes do not play fair because of the way the vowel sound in any syllable is either clear and fair or muddy and murky.

<u>c + -le</u> syllables are always unaccented; they don't play fair, and this can make spelling them tricky. Some folks without much else to do will argue about whether there is or isn't a vowel sound at all in <u>c + -le</u> syllables. Do you say "/ə/ /l/" or just "/l/"? Or is there any difference? At least the first syllable is accented and the vowel sound in it *is* clear and easy to hear.

The schwa (ə) vowel sound that is or isn't heard in the <u>c + -le</u> syllable is mostly or completely covered up by the sound represented by the letter <u>l</u>. We said earlier that the difference between vowel sounds and consonant sounds was that vowels are open sounds and consonants are closed, blocked sounds.

The slippery thing about the /l/ sound is that it is a consonant sound with vowel-like qualities. The /l/ sound doesn't have a crisp beginning and ending like /k/ or /t/ or /d/. For this reason, /l/ is called a **liquid sound**. The muffled schwa vowel sound gets flooded by the liquid <u>l</u> in <u>c + -le</u> syllables.

The *most* annoying thing about <u>c + -le</u> syllables is that *there are many other ways to represent this same /əl/ sound in the English language spelling system*. EEEK!

Exercise 3a

Sort these words based on their spelling at the *end* for the /əl/ sound.

final	angel	nickel	fable	fragile
pencil	local	normal	parcel	medal
bungle	missile	nostril	freckle	evil

c + -le	-il	-ile	-al	-el
freckle	pencil	missile	final	parcel
bungle	nostril	fragile	normal	nickel
fable	evil	fertile ★	medal	angel
pickle ★	April ★	mobile ★	local	cancel ★
uncle ★	pupil ★	hostile ★	equal ★	camel ★
eagle ★	civil ★		tidal ★	shovel ★
			formal ★	

Add three new words to each of the groups. Star (★) the new words you find.

Casey? In **c + -le** syllables where the consonant makes the /k/ sound, you can spell this /k/ sound with **k** (an**kle**), **ck** (ti**ckle**), or **c** (un**cle**).

Fill in the blanks with the letters **k**, **ck**, or **c** to complete these words.

cir_c_le	an_k_le	spar_k_le	bu_ck_le	twin_k_le
pi_ck_le	cy_c_le	sprin_k_le	ici_c_le	fre_ck_le

Duh! As you know, there are 40+ speech sounds in the English language, and they are all marvelous. When these sounds get together, they try to work as a team to create the combined sounds that we call words. This calls for a lot of give and take among the sounds because some sounds are hard to say next to other sounds.

Try saying this line from Dr. Seuss' *Fox in Socks* a few times fast (then ice your tongue):

"Luke Luck likes lakes. Luke's duck likes lakes."

Sounds change a little or a lot because it must be easy for our mouths to say the sequences of sounds.

When the sounds /t/ and /d/ are used in the middle position between an accented vowel and an unaccented vowel, the change is strange. Read these words aloud:

li**tt**le pu**dd**le bo**tt**le i**d**le la**dd**er

What do you notice about what happens? Why can it be tricky to spell these words?

We essentially flap our tongues to produce these sounds; we do not make the /t/ or /d/ sounds that the spelling would lead us to expect. If you try to correctly spell these words by sounding them out, you will not be too successful; they are not spelled the way they sound.

Try it out! Fill in the blanks with the letters **tt**, **dd**, **t**, or **d** to complete these words. (Remember that the first vowel will be short if you add **tt** or **dd**.)

ca_tt_le	pe_dd_le	cra_d_le	ke_tt_le	hur_d/t_le
hu_dd_le	bri_d_le	i_d_le	ri_dd_le	stra_dd_le
ti_t_le	li_tt_le	pu_dd_le	bri_tt_le	la_d_le
bee_t_le	mi_dd_le	bo_tt_le	bun_d_le	ra_tt_le

Unheard Of. Sometimes, the consonant in the **c + -le** syllable is silent. It must be frustrating for these poor letters to show up but not be allowed to speak.

Underline the silent letters in each of these words.

whistle

castle

muscle

hustle

wrestle

A long time ago—in Lesson 6 ("Nose Knows")—we learned that there are three "nosey" consonant sounds that we make by pushing air through our nostrils like fireless dragons. Give an example word for each of these three nose sounds:

Example answers:

/m/ = mumps　　/n/ = noggin　　/ng/ = thing

The back-of-the-nose sound /ng/ is spelled at the end of a word with the letters **ng** (si**ng**). In words that have a syllable break between an **n** and a **g**—or between an **n** and a **k**—the **n** works alone to represent /ng/ (a**n**–gle, a**n**–kle). However, the letter **n** also spells /n/ (ca**n**–dle).

List four short words that use the **ng** spelling to represent the /ng/ sound:

Example answers:

bang　　hang　　bring　　rung

Divide these words into syllables by drawing a vertical line at the syllable break. Then, sort the words based on which nose sound the letter **n** represents.

an/gle	sprin/kle	bun/gle
bun/dle	an/kle	han/dle
dan/gle	crin/kle	un/cle
dwin/dle	sin/gle	kin/dle
wran/gle	man/tle	jun/gle

n = **/ng/**
(as in **bangle**)

angle
single
sprinkle
dangle
bungle
crinkle
wrangle
uncle
ankle
jungle

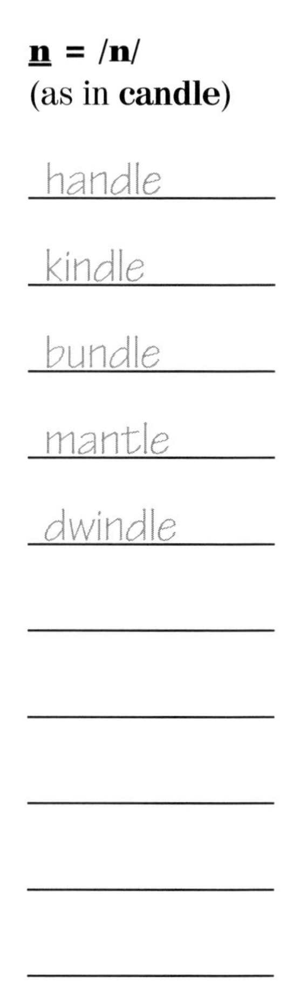

n = **/n/**
(as in **candle**)

handle
kindle
bundle
mantle
dwindle

Work with a small group to list as many <u>c + -le</u> words as you can in these groups.

Example answers:

<u>-kle</u> Words (as in **ankle**)	**<u>-cle</u> Words** (as in **uncle**)	**<u>-gle</u> Words** (as in **single**)	**<u>-tle</u> Words** (as in **title**)
crinkle	bicycle	eagle	cattle
knuckle	circle	angle	title
trickle	article	bugle	little
freckle	cycle	gurgle	battle
pickle	barnacle	giggle	bottle
buckle	icicle	struggle	hurtle
tickle	particle	strangle	turtle

<u>-dle</u> Words (as in **puddle**)	**<u>-ble</u> Words** (as in **table**)	**<u>-ple</u> Words** (as in **apple**)
huddle	cable	people
candle	rumble	staple
needle	humble	dimple
poodle	grumble	ripple
cradle	stumble	topple
fiddle	tremble	simple
cuddle	squabble	cripple

Exercise 9

Take note of these homophones!

Bridal means having to do with a bride.

Bridle is what you put on a horse.

Pedal is something you do on a bicycle.

Peddle means try to sell something on the street, usually person to person.

Petal is part of the blossom of a flower.

Tidal means having to do with the ocean's tides.

Title is the name given to a book, play, story, song, etc.

Use each of these words in a sentence (oral) to share with a partner. On separate sheets of paper, draw simple pictures to illustrate each sentence. Write the homophone in a caption on the picture. Collect these pictures to make a Homophone Picture Dictionary.

Sentence Dictations Use each group of words in a sentence to use for dictation. You can change the words by adding endings if you need to.

Example answers:

1. shingles, steeple, brittle The shingles on the steeple were brittle.

2. turtle, startle, simple A simple paddle noise may startle the turtle off its rock.

3. sparkle, noble, bridle The bridle on the noble horse did sparkle in the sun.

4. cycle, pedal, circle If you pedal your cycle in a circle, you may wobble.

5. disabled, peddler, twinkle The peddler had a twinkle in his eyes when he sold us the disabled bugle.

6. beetle, wobble, little The beetle did wobble a little after it fell off the leafy branch.

Exercise 11

Speed Read Time yourself reading these word-pair sets out loud from left to right on three different days.

bun	bundle	sam	sample	ram	ramble
bog	boggle	can	candle	crack	crackle
purr	purple	spark	sparkle	mar	marble
sir	circle	car	gargle	fur	gurgle
herd	hurdle	lit	little	rid	riddle
cat	cattle	beet	beetle	rat	rattle
sad	saddle	pad	paddle	hand	handle
ride	bridle	tie	title	lad	ladder
sigh	cycle	no	noble	may	maple
bun	bungle	shin	shingle	an	angle

Day 1	**Day 2**	**Day 3**
Time: ________	Time: ________	Time: ________
Errors: ________	Errors: ________	Errors: ________

Finally: Take the Posttest, and record your score here. **Number Correct:** __________

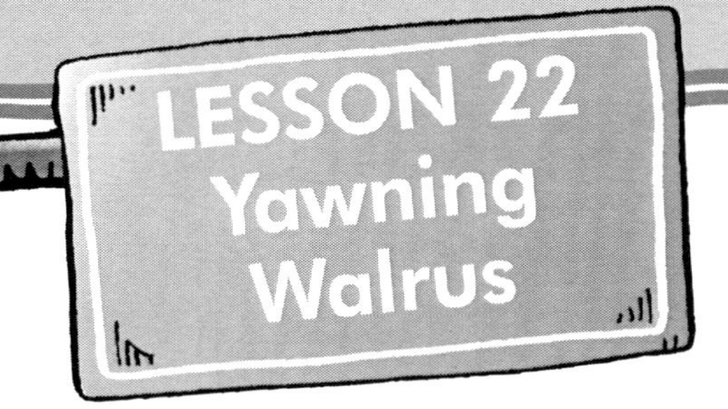

Phonemic Awareness Activities

1. **Identify the Vowel Sound** These words compare and contrast the /ŏ/ (**hot**), /aw/ (**lawn**), and /ō/ (**so**) open vowel sounds. Decide which vowel sound applies to each of these words.

lone /ō/	**tall** /aw/	**scald** /aw/	**poll** /ō/	**Don** /ŏ/
lawn /aw/	**toll** /ō/	**scold** /ō/	**Paul** /aw/	**dawn** /aw/
tot /ŏ/	**drawn** /aw/	**wall** /aw/	**josh** /ŏ/	**chop** /ŏ/
taught /aw/	**drone** /ō/	**doll** /ŏ/	**jaw** /aw/	**chalk** /aw/

2. **Segmentation Activity** Hold up the number of fingers—or show the number of markers—that is equal to the number of sounds (phonemes) in each of these words.

law /l/ /aw/	**lawn** /l/ /aw/ /n/	**dawn** /d/ /aw/ /n/	**drawn** /d/ /r/ /aw/ /n/	**drawl** /d/ /r/ /aw/ /l/	**draw** /d/ /r/ /aw/
saw /s/ /aw/	**sauce** /s/ /aw/ /s/	**saucer** /s/ /aw/ /s/ /er/	**paw** /p/ /aw/	**thaw** /th/ /aw/	**thawed** /th/ /aw/ /d/
earn /er/ /n/	**burn** /b/ /er/ /n/	**auburn** /aw/ /b/ /er/ /n/	**August** /aw/ /g/ /ĭ/ /s/ /t/	**author** /aw/ /th/ /er/	
pa /p/ /ŏ/	**paw** /p/ /aw/	**Paul** /p/ /aw/ /l/	**Saul** /s/ /aw/ /l/	**salt** /s/ /aw/ /l/ /t/	**salted** /s/ /aw/ /l/ /t/ /ĭ/ /d/
it /ĭ/ /t/	**sit** /s/ /ĭ/ /t/	**faucet** /f/ /aw/ /s/ /ĭ/ /t/	**all** /aw/ /l/	**wall** /w/ /aw/ /l/	**walrus** /w/ /aw/ /l/ /r/ /ĭ/ /s/

Phonemic Awareness Activities (Continued)

3. **Deletion Task** Say each word after deleting the identified sound (phoneme).

stall without /s/ | **flaw** without /f/ | **false** without /s/ | **pause** without /z/
drawn without /r/ | **fault** without /t/ | **claws** without /l/ | **small** without /s/
scrawl without /s/ | **slaw** without /l/

4. **Substitution Task** Substitute the first sound with the second sound to make a new word.

haul /h/ – /b/ | **taut** /aw/ – /ŏ/ | **jaw** /j/ – /p/ | **cause** /k/ – /l/
stall /t/ – /m/ | **fawn** /f/ – /l/ | **drawl** /aw/ – /ĭ/ | **yawn** /y/ – /d/
fawn /aw/ – /ĭ/ | **flaw** /aw/ – /ō/ | **sprawl** /p/ – /k/ | **dawn** /aw/ – /ŏ/

5. **Sound Reversals** Reverse the sounds (phonemes) to make a new word (**pit – tip**).

awl – law | **taught – taught** | **gnawed – dawn** | **sauce – sauce**

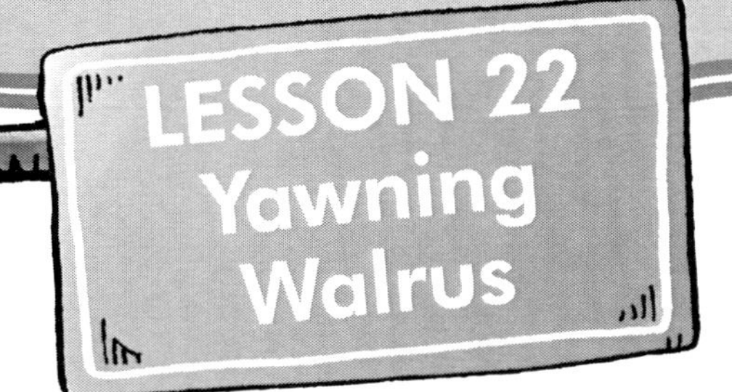

Dictate words in the lesson word list for Pretest and Posttest administration. Modify the number of words as needed.

Lesson 22 Word List

1.	August	13.	all right
2.	thaw	14.	guffaw
3.	also	15.	because
4.	faucet	16.	sprawl
5.	scrawl	17.	coleslaw
6.	awful	18.	unsalted
7.	auburn	19.	falsely
8.	always	20.	yawning
9.	saucer	21.	dawdle
10.	drawn	22.	automatic
11.	autumn	23.	flawless
12.	walrus	24.	authentic

This week, we enter the kingdom of the forgotten and misunderstood vowel sounds. The /aw/ sound is a back, open, awesome sound; it is a jaw-dropping, moaning, "Aw gee, Mom!" kind of sound. The /aw/ sound is like the voice of King Kong climbing the Empire State Building, beating his chest and crooning. It's also interesting to spell.

Spelling Concept: There are several interesting, memorable ways to spell the sound /aw/ in English. You can be helped somewhat by understanding common patterns, including the position in a word or syllable where /aw/ occurs.

Underline the letters in this lesson's spelling words that represent the /aw/ sound, as in **aw**ful and **au**to.

Lesson 22 Word List

1. August
2. thaw
3. also
4. faucet
5. scrawl
6. awful
7. auburn
8. always
9. saucer
10. drawn
11. autumn
12. walrus
13. all right
14. guffaw
15. because
16. sprawl
17. coleslaw
18. unsalted
19. falsely
20. yawning
21. dawdle
22. automatic
23. flawless
24. authentic

Sort this lesson's spelling words by the letters used to spell the /aw/ sound, and then sort the **aw** spelling words by the letters' position within the word.

au = /aw/		**al = /awl/**	
August	faucet	also	always
auburn	saucer	walrus	all right
autumn	because	unsalted	falsely
automatic	authentic		

aw = /aw/

End of word (as in s**aw**)	**End of syllable** (as in cl**aw**-ing)	In a syllable, followed by a consonant **l** (as in **awl**)	**n** (as in **awn**-ing)
thaw	awful	scrawl	drawn
guffaw	dawdle	sprawl	yawning
coleslaw	flawless		

Spelling Concept: Each of the three spellings for the /aw/ sound that we're looking at in this lesson (there are more) are used in certain patterns. You can become an awesome, awe-inspiring, audacious speller by learning these spelling patterns for aw and au.

Auto As you will see, there are many words that start with the letters au. First, list the five study words that *begin* with the au spelling for /aw/. Then, look in a dictionary, and list three new words that begin with au.

Lesson 22 Word List

1. August	7. auburn	13. all right	19. falsely
2. thaw	8. always	14. guffaw	20. yawning
3. also	9. saucer	15. because	21. dawdle
4. faucet	10. drawn	16. sprawl	22. automatic
5. scrawl	11. autumn	17. coleslaw	23. flawless
6. awful	12. walrus	18. unsalted	24. authentic

Study words

August
auburn
autumn
automatic
authentic

New words

____
____
____

Example answers:

auger, auricle, automobile, aurora, audit, auspicious, aught, Australia, augment, author, auditorium

Write a meaningful sentence using as many of these au words as you can.

Answers will vary.

____
____

Raw Paw The **aw** spelling is often found at the end of many common words. List the three study words—and one study word with a root—that end with the **aw** spelling. Then, build as many words as you can that end with **aw**. Remember to try using initial consonant blends to build some of these words.

Study words/root

thaw | guffaw | coleslaw | flawless

Example answers:

s aw	gn aw	p aw	str aw
cl aw	l aw	r aw	dr aw

Middle Muddle It is difficult to always spell the /aw/ sound accurately in the middle of syllables. One helpful pattern is that **aw** inside a syllable is usually followed by an **l** (**awl**) or an **n** (**lawn**). Build words that end with these **awl** and **awn** spellings.

Example answers:

dr awl	cr awl	y awn	dr awn
b awl	spr awl	p awn	f awn
br awl	scr awl	d awn	sp awn

Write a meaningful sentence using as many of the **aw**, **awl**, and **awn** words (from Exercises 3b and 3c) as you can.

Answers will vary.

Awful Sorry, but there are also some words that use **au** before **l** (**haul**) and **n** (**haunt**). Then, there are exceptions—such as **squawk**. The /aw/ sound in this middle position is a trickster. Do you feel lucky? Try completing these words by adding **aw** or **au**. Then, check the spellings in a dictionary, and record how many you got correct.

dr_aw_l	h_au_l	dr_aw_n	h_au_nt
P_au_l	sh_aw_l	p_au_se	p_aw_s
p_aw_n	fl_au_nt	c_au_se	cl_aw_s
f_au_lt	cr_aw_l	l_aw_n	l_au_ndry

Total Correct: _____

All Fall The **al** spelling sometimes represents the /aw/ sound, but it also represents other sounds. Compare the sounds represented by **al** in these words. Underline the /aw/ words.

alto	almost	also	alien	almond	all right
Alex	alone	always	albino	alert	ale

How many other sounds are there? _4_ **(as grouped below)**

Group 1: alto, Alex, albino

Group 2: alien, ale

Group 3: alone, alert

Group 4: almond (silent)

Compounding Your Problems Here are compounding problems to add to your other problems.

1. Give a word example for each of the three ways that compound words can be built.
   Example answers:

   sailboat ______ mix-up ______ White House ______

2. Use a dictionary to find compound words that begin with **all**. List five of them here.
   Example answers:

   all-around ______ all-nighter ______ all clear ______

   all-out ______ all along ______

3. In what form are most of these compound words built?

   The hyphenated form. (Some have a space between words; even fewer are the one-word compound form.)

All Over How many words can you build that end in **all**?
Example answers:

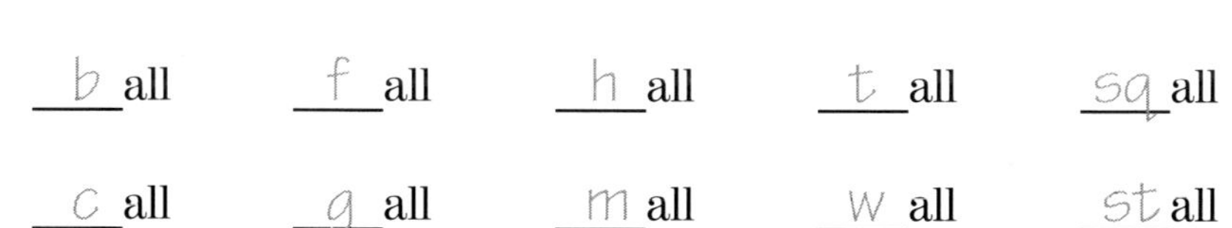

b all　　f all　　h all　　t all　　sq all

c all　　g all　　m all　　w all　　st all

Spelling Concept: Syllables All syllables are built around one vowel sound. When a word has two or more syllables, one syllable is spoken with more stress than the other syllable. That syllable is *accented*—it is easy to identify the vowel sound. *Unaccented* syllables often have a **schwa** sound; the vowel sound is muffled and indistinct. These are the parts you cannot sound out. Beware!

Syllable Stall Let's re-pair these syllables.

a. First, read these two groups of syllables:

Group 1	**Group 2**
au flaw wal Au fau au	**less cet thor tumn gust rus**

b. Then, combine the syllables from Group 1 and Group 2 to form six words.

author | flawless | walrus
August | faucet | autumn

c. Read the words you just built. How did the second syllables change?

The second syllables are all unaccented and their vowel sounds have been reduced to schwa. (Notice how the second [Group 2] syllables sound different when they are read in isolation as opposed to when they are read as the second syllable of a word.)

Match one syllable from each column to form words.

daw	ful	dawdle	al	so	also
awe	burn	awesome	all	ready	all ready/already
sau	ning	saucer	al	wrong	almost
aw	cause	awful	al	-day	always
au	some	auburn	all	most	all wrong
be	dle	because	all	-out	all-day
aw	cer	awning	all	ways	all-out
			all	-time	all-time

Word Surgeon Divide these words into syllables by circling the prefix, underlining the roots, and boxing the suffixes.

unsalted **falsely** **flawless** **yawning**

Now, in the first row of lines, list the prefix you circled and two of the suffixes you boxed. Then, build five new words using each of these affixes.

Prefix	Suffix	Suffix
un-	-ed / -ly	-less / -ing

Example answers:

New words

unspoken	stopped/thickly	hopeless/merging
unequal	marinated/richly	hapless/relaxing
unused	approved/nicely	priceless/sprinting
unthankful	applauded/bravely	shameless/digesting
unproven	limited/awfully	timeless/scrawling

Spelling Concept: Homophones Because you know that **homo** means "the same," and **phone** means "sound," you know that homophones are words that sound the same. **Write/right**, **pedal/peddle/petal**, and **billed/build** are examples of homophones. There are so many ways to represent the /aw/ sound in our spelling system that we should certainly expect to have homophones with /aw/.

Same Name Read through these pairs of /aw/ homophones. Then, circle two of the pairs. Use each of the circled pairs in a sentence that demonstrates the different meanings of the homophones. Finally—all of you budding artisans—draw a picture that illustrates one of those homophone pairs to add to your magnificent Homophone Picture Dictionary.

pause/paws	hall/haul	awl/all	bawl/ball
alter/altar	claws/clause	taught/taut	mall/maul

Answers will vary.

1. ____.

2. ____.

Parts of Speech: The **nouns** in this lesson's word list name several things. Nouns can also be names of places (**Austin** and **Albany**) or names for abstract concepts (**fault** or **falsehood**).

Noun Town List all of the "Thing" nouns from this lesson's spelling list. Then, add two new words to the "Place" and "Abstract Idea" columns.

Lesson 22 Word List

1. August	7. auburn	13. all right	19. falsely
2. thaw	8. always	14. guffaw	20. yawning
3. also	9. saucer	15. because	21. dawdle
4. faucet	10. drawn	16. sprawl	22. automatic
5. scrawl	11. autumn	17. coleslaw	23. flawless
6. awful	12. walrus	18. unsalted	24. authentic

Example answers are starred (★).

Thing	Place	Abstract Idea
faucet	New York ★	awe ★
August	Chicago ★	authority ★
saucer		
autumn		
walrus		
coleslaw		
thaw		
scrawl		
sprawl		
guffaw		

Parts of Speech: Verbs name action. They are *doing* words.

Let's Get Verbal Find four verbs in your study words. Then, complete each sentence by telling where, why, what, when, how, or to whom the action is being done.

Lesson 22 Word List		
1. August	9. saucer	17. coleslaw
2. thaw	10. drawn	18. unsalted
3. also	11. autumn	19. falsely
4. faucet	12. walrus	20. yawning
5. scrawl	13. all right	21. dawdle
6. awful	14. guffaw	22. automatic
7. auburn	15. because	23. flawless
8. always	16. sprawl	24. authentic

Example answers:

Verb	Where, Why, What, When, How, or to Whom
I thaw	meat and poultry in the refrigerator before roasting them in the oven.
I scrawl	messages at night to Mabel because she makes me goofy.
I sprawl	on the couch at night after working hard all day.
I dawdle	by Mabel's window after school, hoping that she'll see me.

Parts of Speech: **Adverbs** are words that describe verbs:

Albert **slowly** *snores*. Ethyl **never** *snores*.

Use the adverbs falsely, always, and also in sentences. Then, draw a line from these adverbs to the actions they refer to in the sentence.

Example answers:

Erma falsely accused me of ignoring her.

Bert always eats with his mouth open to impress his friends.

Merv also eats with his mouth open because he wants to be like Bert.

Dictation Station Study these phrases, idioms, and figures of speech. Be prepared to write them all. After writing them, use the phrases, idioms, and figures of speech in spoken sentences.

automatic pilot	unsalted chips	overdrawn
authentic scrawl	yawning chasm	cup and saucer
flawless walrus	also-ran	awful scrawl
urban sprawl	August vacation	just because

Magic Square Dare Build words using the letters in each of these magic squares.

Magic Square

s	t	h
e	aw	n
r	d	l

Magic Square

g	i	ch
f	au	n
h	l	t

Speed Read Time yourself on three separate days reading these columns of words out loud from top to bottom. Record your times and errors.

call	lawn	awl	awe	auto
hall	yawn	bawl	law	automobile
ball	fawn	crawl	claw	automatic
fall	pawn	drawl	slaw	automaker
tall	dawn	scrawl	straw	
stall		sprawl		all but
small	thaw		alter	all right
scrawl	draw	all-out	alley	all wrong
	gnaw	all-time	already	all over
awe	straw	all-day	allergy	all out
awful		all-American	Albany	
awesome	salt	all-nighter	alto	draw
awesomely	salted		always	drawn
	unsalted		Albert	dawn

Day 1	Day 2	Day 3
Time: ________	Time: ________	Time: ________
Errors: ________	Errors: ________	Errors: ________

Finally: Take the Posttest, and record your score here. **Number Correct:** __________

Phonemic Awareness Activities

1. **Identify the Vowel Sound** These words compare and contrast the /ou/ (**cow**) vowel sound with the /ŏ/ (**hot**), /ō/ (**so**), and /aw/ (**lawn**) vowel sounds. Decide which vowel sound applies to each of these words.

plow /ou/	**pow** /ou/	**lot** /ŏ/	**ought** /aw/	**rout** /ou/
slow /ō/	**paw** /aw/	**lout** /ou/	**out** /ou/	**rot** /ŏ/
no /ō/	**pond** /ŏ/	**foul** /ou/	**clone** /ō/	**shot** /ŏ/
now /ou/	**pound** /ou/	**fall** /aw/	**clown** /ou/	**shout** /ou/

2. **Segmentation Activity** Hold up the number of fingers—or show the number of markers—that is equal to the number of sounds (phonemes) in each of these words.

out /ou/ /t/	**ouch** /ou/ /ch/	**pouch** /p/ /ou/ /ch/	**grouch** /g/ /r/ /ou/ /ch/	**growl** /g/ /r/ /ou/ /l/	**growled** /g/ /r/ /ou/ /l/ /d/	
crow /k/ /r/ /ō/	**crouch** /k/ /r/ /ou/ /ch/	**couch** /k/ /ou/ /ch/	**slow** /s/ /l/ /ō/	**slouch** /s/ /l/ /ou/ /ch/	**pouch** /p/ /ou/ /ch/	**ouch** /ou/ /ch/
cow /k/ /ou/	**count** /k/ /ou/ /n/ /t/	**account** /a/ /k/ /ou/ /n/ /t/	**win** /w/ /ĭ/ /n/	**wind** /w/ /ĭ/ /n/ /d/	**window** /w/ /ĭ/ /n/ /d/ /ō/	
ounce /ou/ /n/ /s/	**bounce** /b/ /ou/ /n/ /s/	**loud** /l/ /ou/ /d/	**cloud** /k/ /l/ /ou/ /d/	**clouded** /k/ /l/ /ou/ /d/ /ĭ/ /d/	**mouse** /m/ /ou/ /s/	**blouse** /b/ /l/ /ou/ /s/
town /t/ /ou/ /n/	**frown** /f/ /r/ /ou/ /n/	**round** /r/ /ou/ /n/ /d/	**frowned** /f/ /r/ /ou/ /n/ /d/	**rout** /r/ /ou/ /t/	**trout** /t/ /r/ /ou/ /t/	**sprout** /s/ /p/ /r/ /ou/ /t/

Phonemic Awareness Activities (Continued)

3. **Deletion Task** Say each word after deleting the identified sound (phoneme).

shout without /sh/	**crow** without /k/	**pounce** without /p/	**couch** without /ch/
plow without /l/	**crouch** without /r/	**brown** without /n/	**spout** without /s/
foul without /f/	**window** without /d/	**brow** without /r/	**sprout** without /r/

4. **Substitution Task** Substitute the first sound with the second sound to make a new word.

now /n/ – /b/	**fond** /ŏ/ – /ou/	**house** /h/ – /m/	**hoe** /ō/ – /ou/
south /s/ – /m/	**fall** /aw/ – /ou/	**crowd** /d/ – /n/	**foul** /f/ – /h/
vowel /v/ – /t/	**no** /ō/ – /ou/	**mound** /m/ – /b/	**pond** /ŏ/ – /ou/
pounce /p/ – /b/	**clone** /ō/ – /ou/	**powder** /p/ – /ch/	**trot** /ŏ/ – /ou/
spout /p/ – /k/	**prod** /ŏ/ – /ou/	**crown** /r/ – /l/	**ought** /aw/ – /ou/

5. **Sound Reversals** Reverse the sounds (phonemes) to make a new word (**pit – tip**).

ouch – chow	**dowel – loud**	**towel – lout**
tower – rout	**noun – noun**	

Dictate words in the lesson word list for Pretest and Posttest administration. Modify the number of words as needed.

Lesson 23 Word List

1.	ouch	13.	around
2.	plow	14.	rowdy
3.	crow	15.	frown
4.	flower	16.	burrow
5.	window	17.	towel
6.	crouch	18.	pounce
7.	ounce	19.	unknown
8.	growl	20.	ousted
9.	brown	21.	mountain
10.	amount	22.	allowed
11.	outgrown	23.	thousand
12.	drowsy	24.	scowling

Spelling Concept: The sound /ou/ (as in **cow**) is a **diphthong**.

The word **diphthong** comes from Greek, and it means "two voices" or "two sounds." If you watch a friend or your cat say "Meow," you will notice how much work the mouth has to do. Try saying **meow** with your lips perfectly still. Har-har! When you say /ou/, your mouth slides and puckers. That's why it's a diphthong! The /ou/ sound is suitable for cats and boo-boos.

The two ways we spell the /ou/ sound are **ow** and **ou**. The **ow** spelling can also represent the /ō/ (as in **blow**) sound.

Exercise 1

In this lesson's word list, underline the letters that represent the /ou/ sound (as in c**ow** and **ou**t), and box the letters that make the /ō/ sound (as in sn**ow**).

Sort this lesson's words by ou and ow spelling groups. Then, sort each group according to sound and letter position within a word, as indicated. Star (★) any words that fit into more than one group.

Lesson 23 Word List

1. ouch	9. brown	17. towel
2. plow	10. amount	18. pounce
3. crow	11. outgrown	19. unknown
4. flower	12. drowsy	20. ousted
5. window	13. around	21. mountain
6. crouch	14. rowdy	22. allowed
7. ounce	15. frown	23. thousand
8. growl	16. burrow	24. scowling

ou Words

ouch	mountain
crouch	thousand
ounce	
amount	
outgrown ★	
around	
pounce	
ousted	

ow Words

plow	rowdy
crow	frown
flower	burrow
window	towel
growl	unknown
brown	allowed
outgrown ★	scowling
drowsy	

ou = /ou/

Beginning of a Word
(as in **out**)

ouch
ounce
outgrown ★
ousted

Inside a Word or Syllable
(as in **loud** or **loud-ly**)

crouch
amount
around
pounce
mountain
thousand

ow = /ou/

End of a Word or Syllable
(as in **cow** or **cow-ard**)

plow
flower
drowsy
rowdy
towel

Inside a Word or Syllable
(as in **town** or **town-ship**)

growl
brown
frown
scowling
allowed

ow = /ō/

End of a Word or Syllable
(as in **blow** or **blow-ing**)

crow
window
burrow

Inside a Word or Syllable
(as in **bowl** or **bowl-er**)

outgrown ★
unknown

Spelling Concept: As you saw in Exercise #2, the **ou** spelling for /ou/ is used primarily in the front position of words, and the **ow** spelling for /ou/ is used primarily at the end of words and syllables. In the middle position—that is, inside words and syllables—it is more difficult to determine the correct spelling.

Fill in the blanks to form words ending with **ow**. Then, underline the words in which **ow** represents /ou/ (as in **cow**), and box the words in which **ow** represents /ō/ (as in **blow**).

Example answers:

n ow	br ow	[l ow]	[sl ow]	pl ow	[kn ow]
h ow	ch ow	w ow	[t ow]	[st ow]	br ow

Exercise 4

The ow spelling is also used at the end of syllables inside words. Match a Group 1 syllable to a Group 2 syllable to form five words.

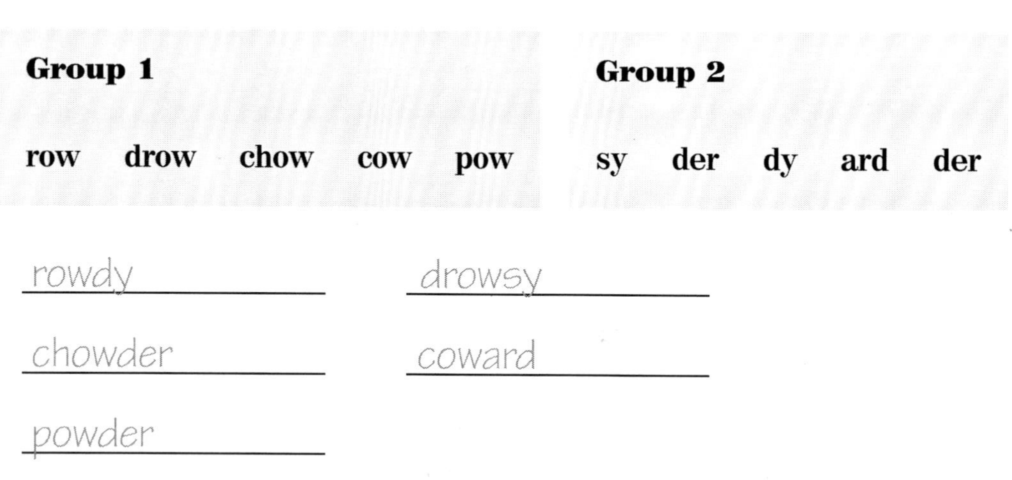

Group 1	Group 2
row drow chow cow pow	sy der dy ard der

rowdy
drowsy
chowder
coward
powder

There is a group of common words in which the <u>ow</u> spelling ends a first syllable, and the second syllable is the suffix **<u>-er</u>** or **<u>-el</u>**. Complete these words with **<u>-er</u>** or **<u>-el</u>**.

flow*er*	tow*el*	tow*er*	show*er*
vow*el*	pow*er*	dow*el*	trow*el*

Most of the words that start with <u>ou</u> use the Anglo-Saxon prefix **<u>out-</u>**, which means "in a manner that exceeds and surpasses." Use a dictionary to find 12 words built with the prefix **<u>out-</u>**.

out__________	out__________	out__________	out__________
out__________	out__________	out__________	out__________
out__________	out__________	out__________	out__________

Example answers:

outfit	out loud	outlast
outsmart	outboard	outstanding
outdoor	outlook	outlaw
outlive	outwit	outbreak
outpost	outlet	outside
outpace	outrun	out-of-sight

Spelling Concept In the middle position—that is, inside syllables—the **ow** spelling is used most of the time before a single **n** (as in **town**) or **l** (as in **howl**). This **ow** spelling can represent both /ou/ (as in **town**) and /ō/ (as in **blown**).

Fill in the blanks to form words ending with **-owl** and **-own**. Then, underline the words in which the **ow** is pronounced /ou/, and box the words in which **ow** is pronounced /ō/.

Example answers:

f owl	d own	br own	[bl own]
[b owl]	[fl own]	cr own	fr own
gr owl	cl own	[sh own]	g own

Spelling Concept Most words use the **ou** spelling to represent /ou/ inside words and syllables.

Fill in the blanks to complete these words, using the **ou** spelling for the /ou/ sound.

Example answers:

c ount	p ouch	st out	bl ouse
m ount	sl ouch	p out	h ouse
acc ount	c ouch	tr out	m ouse

Put It All Together By learning the three rules for spelling both the /aw/ (as in **saw**) and /ou/ (as in **cow**) sounds, you—yes, you!—can rule over /aw/ and /ou/.

1. If the sound is in the **beginning** position (at the front of a word), use:
   ou for /ou/ (**out**)
   au for /aw/ (**au–to**)

2. If the sound is in the **middle** of a word or a syllable, *usually* use:

   a. **ou** for /ou/ (**mouse**, **house–ful**)
   au for /aw/ (**cause**, **be–cause**)

   However, if the sound is followed by only a single **n** or **l**, use:

   b. **ow** for /ou/ (**brown**, **howl**) and /ō/ (**bowl**, **own**)
   aw for /aw/ (**lawn**, **crawl**)

3. If the sound is at the **end** of a word or a syllable, use:
   ow for /ou/ (**cow**) and /ō/ (**crow**, **be–low**)
   aw for /aw/ (**saw**, **out–law**)

Fill in the blanks with **au**, **aw**, **ou**, or **ow**. Then, indicate which rule number (1, 2, or 3) you applied for your spelling. Then, read the words you have made.

	Rule		Rule		Rule		Rule
ou ch	1	pl ow	3	au thor	1	bl ow	3
fl ow er	3	cr ou ch	2a	br ow n	2b	gr ow	3
am ou nt	2a	r ow dy	3	ou nce	1	gr ow l	2b
fr ow n	2b	dr ow sy	3	wind ow	3	ou tgr ow n	1, 2b
ar ou nd	2a	p ow er	3	unkn ow n	2b	p ou nce	2a

Spelling Concept: Syllable Review Each syllable is built around one vowel sound. When a word has two or more syllables, one syllable is said with more stress. That syllable is *accented*. Unaccented syllables often don't play fair; the *unaccented* vowel sound is often disguised as the **schwa** sound. Beware of these schwa syllables!

Read each syllable, then the combined word. Underline the syllable in each word that contains the unaccented, muffled schwa vowel sound.

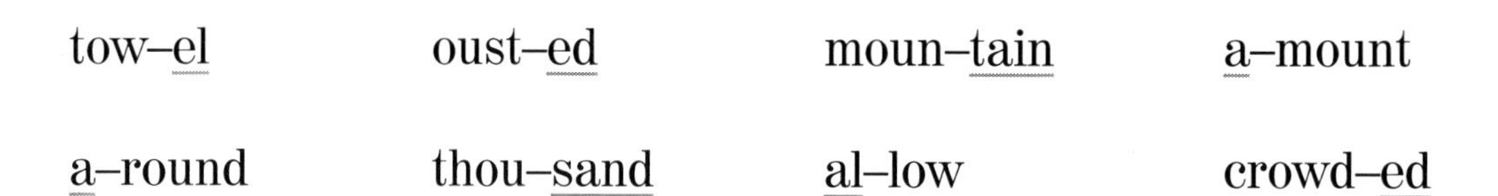

tow–el	oust–ed	moun–tain	a–mount
a–round	thou–sand	al–low	crowd–ed

Syllable Re-Pair Combine the syllables from Group 1 and Group 2 to form five words.

Group 1

win out drow bur un

Group 2

row dow known grown sy

window ______ outgrown ______

drowsy ______ burrow ______

unknown ______

Spelling Concept: Homophone Home There are several ways to represent the /ou/ and /ō/ sounds in our spelling system, so it's not surprising that an awful lot of homophones share these sounds.

Exercise 12

Same Name Read through these sets of /ou/ and /ō/ homophones. Then, circle two of the sets. Use each set in a sentence that demonstrates the different meanings of the homophones. Then, illustrate at least one pair for your Homophone Picture Dictionary.

flour – flower	fowl – foul	groan – grown	bow – bough
hour – our	rose – rows	brows – browse	allowed – aloud

Answers will vary.

1. ______________________________

____

2. ______________________________

____

Parts of speech: Adjectives modify nouns.

Picture This Use four adjectives from this lesson's word list to describe something.

Lesson 23 Word List

1. ouch	9. brown	17. towel
2. plow	10. amount	18. pounce
3. crow	11. outgrown	19. unknown
4. flower	12. drowsy	20. ousted
5. window	13. around	21. mountain
6. crouch	14. rowdy	22. allowed
7. ounce	15. frown	23. thousand
8. growl	16. burrow	24. scowling

Example answers:

	Adjective	**Noun**		**Adjective**	**Noun**
The	brown	cow	The	drowsy	cat
The	rowdy	students	The	scowling	teacher

Parts of Speech: The **nouns** in this lesson's word list are things. Nouns can also be names of people (**Bert**, **Mabel**), places (**Austin**, **Albany**), or abstract ideas (**beauty**, **courage**).

Noun Town Split the nouns in this lesson's word list into groups. Give a title for each group based on a shared quality that sets each group apart.

Lesson 23 Word List

1. ouch	9. brown	17. towel
2. plow	10. amount	18. pounce
3. crow	11. outgrown	19. unknown
4. flower	12. drowsy	20. ousted
5. window	13. around	21. mountain
6. crouch	14. rowdy	22. allowed
7. ounce	15. frown	23. thousand
8. growl	16. burrow	24. scowling

Example answers:

Title:	**Title:**	**Title:**
Great Outdoors	House Items	Measures
plow	window	ounce
flower	towel	amount
mountain		
crow		
burrow		

Parts of Speech: Verbs name actions. They are *doing* words.

Let's Get Verbal Select three verbs from this lesson's word list. Then, use each verb to complete a sentence by telling where, why, what, when, how, or to whom the action is being done.

Lesson 23 Word List

1. ouch	9. brown	17. towel
2. plow	10. amount	18. pounce
3. crow	11. outgrown	19. unknown
4. flower	12. drowsy	20. ousted
5. window	13. around	21. mountain
6. crouch	14. rowdy	22. allowed
7. ounce	15. frown	23. thousand
8. growl	16. burrow	24. scowling

Example answers:

Verb	Where, Why, What, When, How, or to Whom
I plow	my fields in the spring with my horse.
I growl	out my window at night to scare away the raccoons.
I pounce	on mice in the kitchen when they least expect it.

Multi-Use: Split Personality Words Many words carry several meanings and uses. When using these words in a sentence, you can tell the reader which meaning to choose.

Complete each of these sentences. Then, indicate if the **bold** word was used as a noun (**n**) or a verb (**v**).

Example answers:

	n/v
The **burrow** was deep and cozy.	n
They **burrowed** under the fence.	v
The **crow** screeched all morning, using three different calls to bug us.	n
The mother **crowed** about how wonderful her darling daughter was.	v
The **amount** was just right.	n
You may **amount** to a hill of beans if you keep up the nonsense.	v
The **towel** was used to mop up the slop that spilled from the dog's dish.	n
Towel right off before you come in the kitchen.	v

Dictation Station From dictation, write these phrases, idioms, and figures of speech—and other expressive jewels that might come to your brilliant mind—that use this lesson's spelling words.

Lesson 23 Word List

1. ouch	7. ounce	13. around	19. unknown
2. plow	8. growl	14. rowdy	20. ousted
3. crow	9. brown	15. frown	21. mountain
4. flower	10. amount	16. burrow	22. allowed
5. window	11. outgrown	17. towel	23. thousand
6. crouch	12. drowsy	18. pounce	24. scowling

as the crow flies

flower power

out the window

brownout

a smile is a frown upside-down

an ounce of prevention, a pound of cure

no parking allowed

unknown source

Magic Squares Build words using the letters in each of these magic squares.

Magic Square

b	f	er
l	ow	n
s	p	c

Magic Square

h	FREE consonant	ch
t	ou	r
s	e	th

Speed Read Thunker wrote this journal entry after waking up from a nap under an apple tree on the hill behind his farm. Time yourself and track your errors on three separate days reading out loud his piece about the divine bovine, Oaf.

Oaf, the Proud Cow

Oaf, my cow, is a proud cow because she can outkick, outsmart, outeat, and outproduce all the cows in the county. Oaf has a rump that is stout and a nice brown snout. She is outstanding, and she is out standing in the meadow below, scouring for tender sprouts and wildflower chow. While Oaf browses, a small sparrow sits in the willow whistling "In a Mellow Tone," making the cow and me drowsy. Way below, growling in the mud and water, the grouchy sow Sid slouches and snorts, all out of sorts. The sounds of Oaf chomping down stalk-and-sprout coleslaw, the mellow sparrow warbling a song, and Sid burrowing her snout in the brown ground are carried by a low wind, blowing across the mountain meadow, to my ears, to you.

Challenge Activities

1. How many words with the /ou/ sound did you find? 35
2. How many words with the /ō/ sound did you find? 19

Note:
—The 35 /ou/ sounds are marked with thin underlines.
—The 19 /ō/ sounds (including the o in Oaf in the title) are marked with thick underlines. (The o in outproduce does not make an /ō/ sound; this o is a schwa.)

Day 1	Day 2	Day 3
Time: ______	Time: ______	Time: ______
Errors: ______	Errors: ______	Errors: ______

Finally: Take the Posttest, and record your score here. **Number Correct:** ________

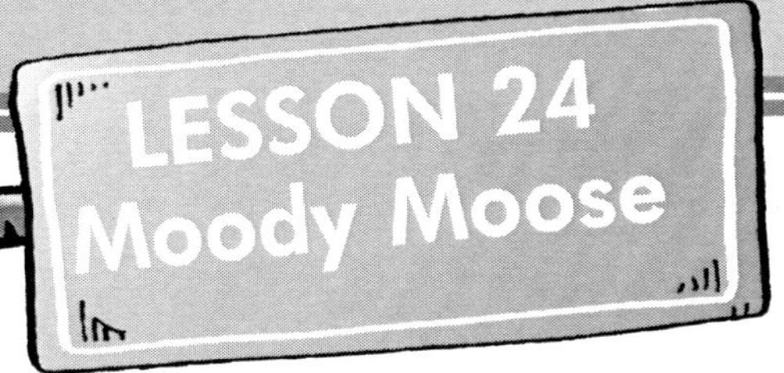

Phonemic Awareness Activities

1. **Segmentation Activity** Hold up the number of fingers—or show the number of markers—that is equal to the number of sounds (phonemes) in each of these words.

flew	**flute**	**fluted**	**two**	**tune**	**tuna**	
/f/ /l/ /ū/	/f/ /l/ /ū/ /t/	/f/ /l/ /ū/ /t/ /ĭ/ /d/	/t/ /ū/	/t/ /ū/ /n/	/t/ /ū/ /n/ /ŭ/	

boot	**boost**	**booster**	**Lou**	**glue**	**gloom**	**gloomy**
/b/ /ū/ /t/	/b/ /ū/ /s/ /t/	/b/ /ū/ /s/ /t/ /er/	/l/ /ū/	/g/ /l/ /ū/	/g/ /l/ /ū/ /m/	/g/ /l/ /ū/ /m/ /ē/

soup	**super**	**superb**	**superbly**
/s/ /ū/ /p/	/s/ /ū/ /p/ /er/	/s/ /ū/ /p/ /er/ /b/	/s/ /ū/ /p/ /er/ /b/ /l/ /ē/

at	**too**	**tattoo**	**tattooed**	**car**	**cart**	**tune**	**cartoon**
/ă/ /t/	/t/ /ū/	/t/ /ă/ /t/ /ū/	/t/ /ă/ /t/ /ū/ /d/	/k/ /ar/	/k/ /ar/ /t/	/t/ /ū/ /n/	/k/ /ar/ /t/ /ū/ /n/

coo	**clue**	**clueless**	**rue**	**true**	**intrude**
/k/ /ū/	/k/ /l/ /ū/	/k/ /l/ /ū/ /l/ /ĭ/ /s/	/r/ /ū/	/t/ /r/ /ū/	/i/ /n/ /t/ /r/ /ū/ /d/

new	**renew**	**renewed**	**rue**	**crew**	**screw**	**unscrew**
/n/ /ū/	/r/ /ē/ /n/ /ū/	/r/ /ē/ /n/ /ū/ /d/	/r/ /ū/	/k/ /r/ /ū/	/s/ /k/ /r/ /ū/	/u/ /n/ /s/ /k/ /r/ /ū/

Lou	**glue**	**igloo**	**moo**	**smooth**	**smoothed**
/l/ /ū/	/g/ /l/ /ū/	/ĭ/ /g/ /l/ /ū/	/m/ /ū/	/s/ /m/ /ū/ /th/	/s/ /m/ /ū/ /th/ /d/

Phonemic Awareness Activities (Continued)

2. **Deletion Task** Say each word after deleting the identified sound (phoneme).

stew without /s/	**flute** without /f/	**groove** without /v/	**flute** without /t/
gloom without /g/	**roost** without /s/	**clue** without /k/	**stoop** without /t/
blue without /l/	**igloo** without /ĭ/	**screw** without /s/	**troop** without /p/

3. **Substitution Task** Substitute the first sound with the second sound to make a new word.

clue /k/ – /f/	**gloom** /g/ – /b/	**chew** /ch/ – /m/	**stoop** /t/ – /k/
troop /p/ – /th/	**groove** /g/ – /p/	**glue** /g/ – /b/	**boot** /b/ – /s/
dude first /d/ – /ch/	**croon** /k/ – /p/	**tooth** /t/ – /b/	**group** /g/ – /t/

4. **Sound Reversals** Reverse the sounds (phonemes) to make a new word (**pit – tip**).

tube – boot	**noose – soon**	**spool – loops**	**mood – doom**
newt – tune	**lute – tool**	**zoo – ooze**	**Luke – cool**

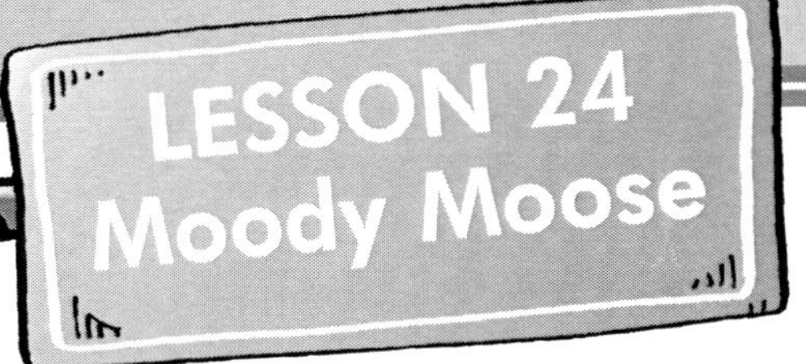

Dictate words in the lesson word list for Pretest and Posttest administration. Modify the number of words as needed.

Lesson 24 Word List

1.	**flute**	13.	**superb**
2.	**tuna**	14.	**voodoo**
3.	**droop**	15.	**mildew**
4.	**untrue**	16.	**gloomy**
5.	**group**	17.	**student**
6.	**cartoon**	18.	**dilute**
7.	**prune**	19.	**overdue**
8.	**Hindu**	20.	**rooster**
9.	**renew**	21.	**intrude**
10.	**igloo**	22.	**tattoo**
11.	**clueless**	23.	**bluegrass**
12.	**smooth**	24.	**nincompoop**

Irregular words:

to/too/two and other homophones

Spelling Concept: The sound /ū/ is spelled with **oo**, **u**, **ew**, **ue**, **ou**, and **u(consonant)e**, which we shall abbreviate as **u**(**c**)**e**.

This week's study words all have an /ū/ (as in **moo**) sound. Different letter patterns spell this sound depending on the position, or where in a word, you hear /ū/.

Underline the letter or letter patterns in this lesson's study words that represent the /ū/ sound. (Do not include the irregular words.) Then, sort the words into the different groups based on the spelling of the /ū/ sound.

Lesson 24 Word List

1. flute
2. tuna
3. droop
4. untrue
5. group
6. cartoon
7. prune
8. Hindu
9. renew
10. igloo
11. clueless
12. smooth
13. superb
14. voodoo
15. mildew
16. gloomy
17. student
18. dilute
19. overdue
20. rooster
21. intrude
22. tattoo
23. bluegrass
24. nincompoop

Irregular words: to/too/two and other homophones

/ū/ = **oo** (as in m**oo**)

- droop
- cartoon
- igloo
- smooth
- voodoo
- gloomy
- rooster
- tattoo
- nincompoop
- proof ★
- choose ★
- shampoo ★
- kangaroo ★

/ū/ = **u** (as in t**u**ba)

- tuna
- Hindu
- superb
- student
- rumor ★
- fluid ★
- Susan ★
- stupid ★
- tulip ★
- scuba ★

/ū/ = **u(c)e** (as in t**ube**)

- flute
- prune
- dilute
- intrude
- include ★
- truce ★
- rule ★
- reduce ★
- salute ★
- June ★
- rude ★
- pollute ★

/ū/ = **ue** (as in tr**ue**)

- untrue
- clueless
- overdue
- bluegrass
- glue ★
- blue ★
- due ★
- Sue ★
- flue ★
- revenue ★

/ū/ = **ew** (as in n**ew**)

- renew
- mildew
- stew ★
- crew ★
- dew ★
- sewer ★
- flew ★

/ū/ = **ou** (as in s**ou**p)

- group
- croup ★
- recoup ★

Exercise 2

Word Find Add two or more different words to each group above. Put a star (★) next to the words you add.

Example answers are starred (★).

Exercise 3

Alphabet Soup Write each set of words in alphabetical order.

a b c d e f g h i j k l m n o p q r s t u v w x y z

Set 1:

droop cartoon bluegrass
dilute clueless

1. bluegrass
2. cartoon
3. clueless
4. dilute
5. droop

Set 2:

tuna prune untrue renew
superb voodoo rooster
tattoo smooth student

1. prune
2. renew
3. rooster
4. smooth
5. student
6. superb
7. tattoo
8. tuna
9. untrue
10. voodoo

Spelling Concept: The way we spell the /ū/ sound in words is somewhat predictable, based on where that sound occurs within the word.

Divide your study words into syllables. (Do not include the irregular words.) Then, sort the words according to the spelling patterns listed on the next three pages. Finally, find at least two other words in a dictionary or a book that fit each pattern. Put a star (★) next to the words you add.

Lesson 24 Word List

1. flute	13. su/perb
2. tu/na	14. voo/doo
3. droop	15. mil/dew
4. un/true	16. gloom/y
5. group	17. stu/dent
6. car/toon	18. di/lute
7. prune	19. o/ver/due
8. Hin/du	20. roos/ter
9. re/new	21. in/trude
10. ig/loo	22. tat/too
11. clue/less	23. blue/grass
12. smooth	24. nin/com/poop

Irregular words: to/too/two and other homophones

Exercise 4 (Continued).

Lesson 24 Word List			
1. flute	7. prune	13. superb	19. overdue
2. tuna	8. Hindu	14. voodoo	20. rooster
3. droop	9. renew	15. mildew	21. intrude
4. untrue	10. igloo	16. gloomy	22. tattoo
5. group	11. clueless	17. student	23. bluegrass
6. cartoon	12. smooth	18. dilute	24. nincompoop

Irregular words: to/too/two and other homophones

May Webster be with you! There are three pattern choices:

Pattern 1: Final /ū/

Open to U In words with more than one syllable—that is, when /ū/ is heard *at the end of a syllable inside a word*—it is usually spelled with an **open u** (**tu**–**ba**). However, a few words end with a single, **open u** (**to–fu**).

Open u Words

tu-na	tu-tu ★
Hin-du	du-et ★
su-perb	su-crose ★
stu-dent	

Example answers are starred (★).

Smooth Team The vowel teams **ue** (**due**), **ew** (**grew**), and **oo** (**shampoo**) are also usually found at the *end of syllables, both inside and at the end of words*.

ue Words	**ew Words**	**oo Words**
un-true	re-new	ig-loo
clue-less	mil-dew	tat-too
o-ver-due	flew ★	voo-doo
blue-grass	stew ★	too ★
glue ★	drew ★	sham-poo ★
blue ★		

Pattern 2: BabOOn in the Middle

When /ū/ is heard *inside a syllable before a consonant sound*, it is spelled one of these three ways:

Vowel Team oo (as in **cool**, **moon**)	**u(c)e Spelling** (as in **rude**)	**Vowel Team ou** (as in **soup**)
droop	flute	group
car-toon	prune	youth ★
smooth	di-lute	troupe ★
gloom-y	in-trude	
roost-er	tune ★	
nin-com-poop	dune ★	
booth ★	dude ★	
doom ★		
loop ★		

Example answers are starred (★).

Exercise 4 (Continued)

Lesson 24 Word List

1. flute	7. prune	13. superb	19. overdue
2. tuna	8. Hindu	14. voodoo	20. rooster
3. droop	9. renew	15. mildew	21. intrude
4. untrue	10. igloo	16. gloomy	22. tattoo
5. group	11. clueless	17. student	23. bluegrass
6. cartoon	12. smooth	18. dilute	24. nincompoop

Irregular words: to/too/two and other homophones

Pattern 3: That's Odd

Challenge Activity No spelling lesson is complete without at least a few truly oddball spelling patterns. Here are two for /ū/. Since none of the study words in this lesson use these spelling patterns, find three words that *do*!

ui (as in **fruit**)	**o** (as in **do**)
suit ★	to ★
juice ★	who ★
bruise ★	two ★
cruise ★	undo ★

Example answers are starred (★).

There are quite a few simple words with the /ū/ sound spelled __oo__. Complete these words by filling in the blanks. Then, write your own "loopy" sentence using one set of four rhyming words.

d oom	s oon	sch ool	tr oop
r oom	n oon	c ool	wh oop
l oom	l oon	st ool	l oop
b oom	m oon	p ool	dr oop

Sentence:

____

____

____

Example answers:

I felt a sense of doom when the room with the loom went "Boom!"

Soon after noon, we sent a loon to the moon.

After school, it's cool to sit on a stool by the pool and drool like a fool.

The troop let out a whoop when the base hit did a loop and a droop into center field.

Spelling Concept: Super-Duper Construction Zone We have learned that Anglo-Saxon words are built by compounding. Sometimes, Latin and Anglo-Saxon word parts get combined into compounds.

One of this week's spelling words—**superb**—comes from the Latin prefix **super-**, which means "over, above, in addition, or on top." The **b** in **superb** comes from the Latin **bus**, meaning "to be." **Superb** means "to be super"! Superb! (Note that the word is NOT **supper**.)

Because the word/prefix **super-** means "over, above, in addition, or on top," it is similar to a group of words that are called **prepositions**. A **position** is a place, and the prefix **pre-** means "before." So, a **pre-position** is a word *placed before* something. Prepositions tell us *where* stuff is. **Over**, **under**, **by**, **to**, and **in** are all prepositions. There are a zillion Anglo-Saxon compound words built using prepositions (like **overdue**). Even though the prefix **super-** comes from the Latin language stream, there are also a zillion compound words built with **super-**. Are you a supersmart, supercool, supersweet superperson?

Use a dictionary to find compound words that use the prepositions **over** and **under**, and the prefix **super-**. See how many words you can list in ten minutes.

Example answers:

over	**under**	**super-**
overcast	understand	superstition
overdue	underdone	superhuman
overgrown	underline	superhighway
overlook	undertake	supernatural
overcome	undercut	superstar
overthrow	undertow	superfine
overwhelm	underhand	supercharged
overtake	underdog	supervision
overlap	underestimate	superficial
overboard	underbrush	supersede

Underline the prefixes in these words. Then, match each prefix with its given meaning. Finally, list two new words that use each prefix.

protrude untrue intrude renew

Example answers:

un-	"not"	unscrew	undone
re-	"back, again"	report	retune
pro-	"forward"	propel	prolong
in-	"into, not"	indent	indirect

The Latin root trude means "to force or push." Use each of these words—built using this root with a prefix—in a sentence that demonstrates its meaning.

Example answers:

intrude If you intrude onto my property again, I will send my mean rooster after you.

protrude His nose does indeed protrude from his face like a baked potato.

Parting Your Speech Find at least four examples of these parts of speech in this week's spelling list. (Do not include the irregular words.) Star (★) those words that can function as more than one part of speech.

Lesson 24 Word List

1. flute	9. renew	17. student
2. tuna	10. igloo	18. dilute
3. droop	11. clueless	19. overdue
4. untrue	12. smooth	20. rooster
5. group	13. superb	21. intrude
6. cartoon	14. voodoo	22. tattoo
7. prune	15. mildew	23. bluegrass
8. Hindu	16. gloomy	24. nincompoop

Irregular words: to/too/two and other homophones

Nouns	Verbs	Adjectives
flute	droop	untrue
tuna	renew	clueless
cartoon	dilute	superb
igloo	intrude	gloomy
voodoo	group ★	overdue
rooster	prune ★	Hindu ★
student	tattoo ★	smooth ★
nincompoop	smooth ★	bluegrass ★
group ★	mildew ★	
prune ★		
Hindu ★		
tattoo ★		
bluegrass ★		
mildew ★		

Travels with Thunker Being a professor, Thunker has been so poor his whole career that he could hardly keep Bess in biscuits, let alone travel. That's why he loves *Webster*, his dictionary. Thunker lets his fingers do the walking across the globe in *Webster*. He visits far-off lands to snatch words—including some words in this lesson.

Match this lesson's study words with the clues about their origins.

Spanish: **atun** tuna

Louisiana Creole (from French): **voudou** voodoo

Alaskan Inuit: **iglu** igloo

Tahitian (Polynesian): **tatau** tattoo

The following definitions have been added for fun and class discussion.

Tuna—an alteration of the Spanish word *atun*—are large, vigorous scombroid food and sport fishes, including albacore and bluefin tuna. (Scombroid is a suborder of marine bony fishes.) For more, see Exercise #11.

Descended from the French word for "deity or demon," **voodoo** is a religion involving ancestor worship and sorcery, with roots in Africa.

Igloo derives from the Inuit word meaning "house."

Tattoo derives from the Tahitian word meaning "to mark or color the skin." **Tattoo** also descends from Danish *taptoe*, meaning "a rapid, rhythmic tapping."

Something Fishy The word **tuna** refers to several different types of large, bony, vigorous marine (sea) fish. The two most notable tunas—other than Charlie—are the **bluefin** and **albacore**.

Look up the **bluefin** and **albacore** tunas in an encyclopedia or on the Internet. List general information about both. Then, list three ways in which they are similar and three ways in which they are different. Finally, draw each type, and label your drawings.

Bluefin Information	**Albacore Information**
The titan (largest) of tunas.	Much smaller than bluefin.
Can weigh up to 1,400 pounds.	Weigh 40–80 pounds.
Up to 14 feet long.	White meat used as canned tuna.
Endangered due to overfishing.	Travel in large shoals (schools).
Favorite sport fish.	Very prolific; females may deposit
Solitary swimmers.	up to four million eggs.

Similarities

Both are in the mackerel family. Both are sleek and cigar-shaped, built for speed. Both have crescent-shaped tails. Both have many small finlets toward the back part of their bodies. Both must swim to breathe. Both migrate thousands of miles.

Differences

Size: Bluefin are much bigger and heavier than albacore.

Travel dispositions: Bluefin are solitary swimmers; albacore travel in large schools.

Bluefin are endangered; albacore are not.

Spelling Concept: Homophone Home Since you know that homo means "the same" and phone means "sound," you know that homophones are words that sound the same but are spelled differently and have different meanings. Let's fiddle with a few /ū/ homophones.

Read through these sets of /ū/ homophones. Then, circle two of the sets. Use each set of words in a sentence that demonstrates the different meanings of the homophones.

to / too / two	do / dew / due	cereal / serial	stew / Stu
new / knew	loot / lute	blue / blew	flew / flue

Answers will vary.

1. ______________________________

____

____

____

____

2. ______________________________

____

____

____

____

____

____

Speed Read Professor Fuzzy Thunker has tried to be an astute observer of critters, and he's made some journal entries that, sadly, weren't lost. Here's one for you to rue. Time yourself reading this masterpiece out loud on three different days. Record your time and number of errors.

The Sad Story of Stupor Stu, the Moody Moose

Like many moose, the moody moose Stu was a gloomy and obtuse buffoon, meaning he was a loony-tune. He was named Stupor Stu due to the state he was in as he chewed and drooled his way through life. Stu was sweet on a caribou named Sue, who knew Stu from her youth spent in a zoo in Peru. Stu, being an obtuse buffoon, thought that Sue was just a new, improved kind of moose, and he would ruminate on her fine features.

One June, with the moon shining like a luminous lunar balloon, Stu saw Sue and started to croon at first like a loon, but soon like a baboon. He was hoping to make Sue swoon.

Sue remembered Stu as a rude, crude dude with rhubarb breath and mildew on the mind. Sue also knew that most moose were uncouth, so Sue wanted nothing to do with Stu. Stu felt marooned when Sue coolly scooted away, leaving Stu alone to brood in the gloom.

Day 1	**Day 2**
Time: ________	Time: ________
Errors: ________	Errors: ________

Challenge Activity

1. How many /ū/ sounds are in Thunker's story? 76

Finally: Take the Posttest, and record your score here. **Number Correct:** ____________

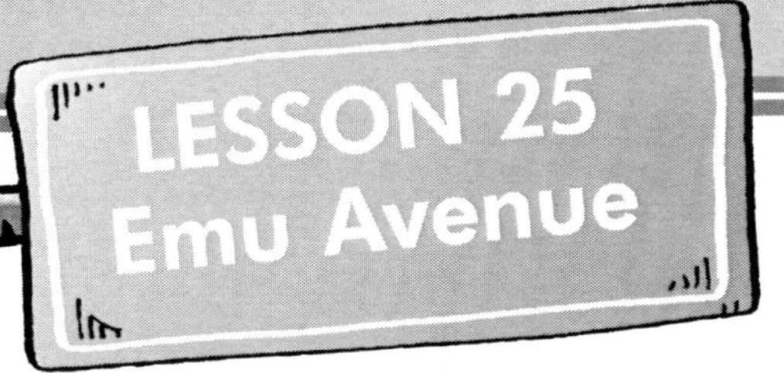

Phonemic Awareness Activities

1. **Segmentation Activity** Hold up the number of fingers—or show the number of markers—that is equal to the number of sounds (phonemes) in each of these words.

you	**few**	**cue**	**cute**	**acute**	**knee**	**puny**
/yū/	/f/ /yū/	/k/ /yū/	/k/ /yū/ /t/	/ŭ/ /k/ /yū/ /t/	/n/ /ē/	/p/ /yū/ /n/ /ē/

pew	**spew**	**spume**	**fume**	**cue**	**skew**	**skewed**
/p/ /yū/	/s/ /p/ /yū/	/s/ /p/ /yū/ /m/	/f/ /yū/ /m/	/k/ /yū/	/s/ /k/ /yū/	/s/ /k/ /yū/ /d/

menu	**venue**	**avenue**	**ten**	**tense**	**utensil**
/m/ /ĕ/ /n/ /yū/	/v/ /ĕ/ /n/ /yū/	/ă/ /v/ /ĕ/ /n/ /yū/	/t/ /ĕ/ /n/	/t/ /ĕ/ /n/ /s/	/yū/ /t/ /ĕ/ /n/ /s/ /ĭ/ /l/

ox	**box**	**jukebox**	**tomb**	**fume**	**perfume**
/ŏ/ /k/ /s/	/b/ /ŏ/ /k/ /s/	/j/ /ū/ /k/ /b/ /ŏ/ /k/ /s/	/t/ /ū/ /m/	/f/ /yū/ /m/	/p/ /er/ /f/ /yū/ /m/

are	**argue**	**argued**	**argument**	**view**	**review**
/ar/	/ar/ /g/ /yū/	/ar/ /g/ /yū/ /d/	/ar/ /g/ /yū/ /m/ /ĕ/ /n/ /t/	/v/ /yū/	/r/ /ē/ /v/ /yū/

2. **Deletion Task** Say each word after deleting the identified sound (phoneme).

cute without /t/
huge without /j/
skew without /s/
skew without /k/
stew without /s/
unite without /yū/

few without /f/
spume without /m/
view without /v/
muse without /m/
preview without /p/
tissue without /t/

Phonemic Awareness Activities (Continued)

3. **Substitution Task** Substitute the first sound with the second sound to make a new word.

cute /yū/ – /ŭ/
view /v/ – /k/
unit /ĭ/ – /ī/

dull /ŭ/ – /yū/
fuel /f/ – /m/
fuzz /ŭ/ – /yū/

union /yū/ – /ŭ/
pewter /yū/ – /ē/
cube /yū/ – /ŭ/

moo /m/ – /ch/
cubic second /k/ – /n/
mull /ŭ/ – /yū/

Dictate words in the lesson word list for Pretest and Posttest administration. Modify the number of words as needed.

Lesson 25 Word List

1.	cute	13.	curfew
2.	puny	14.	dispute
3.	cue	15.	music
4.	few	16.	preview
5.	Utah	17.	argue
6.	spew	18.	acute
7.	rescue	19.	utensil
8.	huge	20.	skew
9.	spume	21.	amusement
10.	bugle	22.	cucumber
11.	view	23.	avenue
12.	humid	24.	perfume

Irregular words: truly, until, their, they

Spelling Concept: The sound /yū/ is spelled with **u**, **ue**, **ew**, and **u(consonant)e**, or **u(c)e**.

This lesson's study words all have a /yū/ (as in **few**) sound: a consonant /y/ before the /ū/. The consonant /y/ is hidden from view; it is usually not spelled with y. (In this sense, the word **you** is unusual.) Many of the same letter patterns that spell /ū/ are also used for /yū/. The position of this sound in a word also helps you know which spelling to choose.

Underline the letter or letter patterns in this lesson's spelling words that represent the /yū/ sound. (Do not include the irregular words.) Then, sort the words into the specified groups.

Lesson 25 Word List

1.	cute	13.	curfew
2.	puny	14.	dispute
3.	cue	15.	music
4.	few	16.	preview
5.	Utah	17.	argue
6.	spew	18.	acute
7.	rescue	19.	utensil
8.	huge	20.	skew
9.	spume	21.	amusement
10.	bugle	22.	cucumber
11.	view	23.	avenue
12.	humid	24.	perfume

Irregular words: truly, until, their, they

/yū/ = **u** (as in **unit**)	/yū/ = **ue** (as in **cue**)	/yū/ = **ew** (as in **few**)	/yū/ = **u(c)e** (as in **cube**)
puny	cue	few	cute
Utah	rescue	spew	huge
bugle	argue	view	spume
humid	avenue	curfew	dispute
music	revenue ★	preview	acute
utensil	value ★	skew	amusement
cucumber	continue ★	review ★	perfume
Cuban ★	hue ★	hew ★	fuse ★
unit ★	imbue ★	nephew ★	use ★
cupid ★	issue ★	pewter ★	abuse ★

Word Find Add two or more different words to each group above. Put a star (★) next to the words you add.

Alphabet Soup Write each set of words in alphabetical order.

a b c d e f g h i j k l m n o p q r s t u v w x y z

Set 1:

cue curfew cucumber cute

1. cucumber
2. cue
3. curfew
4. cute

Set 2:

acute puny few humid
perfume dispute preview
rescue music huge

1. acute
2. dispute
3. few
4. huge
5. humid
6. music
7. perfume
8. preview
9. puny
10. rescue

Spelling Concept: The way we spell the /yū/ sound in words is somewhat predictable, based on where that sound occurs within the word.

Divide this lesson's study words into syllables. (Do not include the irregular words.) Write the spelling words that fit each of the described /yū/ sound patterns on the next two pages. Then, find at least two other words that fit each pattern. Put a star (★) next to the words you add.

Lesson 25 Word List

1. cute	13. cur/few
2. pu/ny	14. dis/pute
3. cue	15. mu/sic
4. few	16. pre/view
5. U/tah	17. ar/gue
6. spew	18. a/cute
7. res/cue	19. u/ten/sil
8. huge	20. skew
9. spume	21. a/muse/ment
10. bu/gle	22. cu/cum/ber
11. view	23. av/e/nue
12. hu/mid	24. per/fume

Irregular words: truly, until, their, they

Exercise 4 (Continued)

Lesson 25 Word List			
1. cute	7. rescue	13. curfew	19. utensil
2. puny	8. huge	14. dispute	20. skew
3. cue	9. spume	15. music	21. amusement
4. few	10. bugle	16. preview	22. cucumber
5. Utah	11. view	17. argue	23. avenue
6. spew	12. humid	18. acute	24. perfume

Irregular words: truly, until, their, they

Pattern 1: At the End

Open to U In words with more than one syllable—that is, when /yū/ is heard *at the end of a syllable inside a word*—/yū/ is usually spelled with an **open u** (**u**–nit). An open **u** is rarely at the end of a word (e-**mu**).

Open u Words

pu-ny	u-ten-sil
U-tah	cu-cum-ber
bu-gle	hu-man ★
hu-mid	cu-pid ★
mu-sic	pu-pil ★

Example answers are starred (★).

Mule Team The vowel teams **<u>ue</u>** (**cue**) and **<u>ew</u>** (**few**), can also represent the sound /yū/ *at the end of words and syllables*.

<u>ue</u> Words	**<u>ew</u> Words**
cue	few
res-cue	spew
ar-gue	view
av-e-nue	pre-view
val-ue ★	skew
is-sue ★	cur-few
con-tin-ue ★	re-view ★
hue ★	neph-ew ★

Pattern 2: In the Middle

When /yū/ is heard *inside a syllable that ends with a consonant sound*, it is spelled with **<u>u</u>(c)<u>e</u>** (m**<u>ule</u>**).

<u>u</u>(c)<u>e</u> Words

cute	per-fume
huge	a-cute
spume	a-buse ★
dis-pute	fuse ★
a-muse-ment	com-pute ★

Example answers are starred (★).

Why are **skew** and **spew** spelled with **<u>ew</u>** while **spume** is spelled with **<u>ume</u>**?

Both **skew** and **spew** end with the /yū/ sound, so they receive an end-position spelling. In the word **spume**, the /yū/ sound is in the middle of the word (inside a syllable that ends with a consonant sound), so it receives a middle-position spelling.

Spelling Concept: The term **synonym** comes from the prefix **syn-**, meaning "the same or similar" and the root **onyma**, meaning "name." A synonym is literally "the same name," or a word that has a similar meaning to another word. Synonyms for the word **fast** are **rapid**, **speedy**, and **swift**.

Skewed Spume Spewed You have to admit that **spew**, **spume**, and **skew** are pretty cool-sounding words. Let's see what they mean.

Spew comes from an ancient Anglo-Saxon word meaning "to spit."

a. **Spew** means "to toss up matter from inside."

b. Find four synonyms for **spew** and list them. Example answers:

gush eject exude vomit

Spume comes from the Latin word meaning "foam."

a. **Spume** means "the frothy matter on liquids."

b. Find four synonyms for **spume** and list them. Example answers:

foam lather froth suds

Skew comes from Anglo-Saxon words meaning "to escape" or "to frighten off."

a. **Skew** means "more developed on one side" or "to distort."

b. Find four synonyms for **skew** and list them. Example answers:

twist distort slant bias

Prefixed Underline the prefixes in these words. Then, match each prefix with its given meaning. Finally, write two new words that use each prefix.

dispute perfume preview amuse rescue compute

Prefix		Example answers: New words	
per-	"throughout"	perfect	permanent
re-	"back, again"	review	return
dis-	"opposite"	dishonest	disagree
pre-	"before"	prevent	prepare
com-	"together, with"	combine	compare
a-	"on, in, at"	ajar	acute

The Latin root pute means "to think." Use each of the following words—built using a prefix from Exercise #6 and the root **pute**—in a sentence that demonstrates its meaning. Indicate the part of speech that the word takes in your sentences.

Example answers:

dispute

We settled the dispute by flipping Herman. (n)

I will not dispute the ruling if I have a chance to be heard. (v)

compute

Ethyl used her calculator to compute how much the project would cost. (v)

Parting Your Speech Find four words in this lesson's spelling list that match each of the following parts of speech. (Do not include the irregular words.) Star (★) those words that can function as more than one part of speech.

Lesson 25 Word List

1. cute	13. curfew
2. puny	14. dispute
3. cue	15. music
4. few	16. preview
5. Utah	17. argue
6. spew	18. acute
7. rescue	19. utensil
8. huge	20. skew
9. spume	21. amusement
10. bugle	22. cucumber
11. view	23. avenue
12. humid	24. perfume

Irregular words: truly, until, their, they

Nouns	Verbs	Adjectives
cue ★	cue ★	cute
Utah	spew	puny
rescue ★	rescue ★	few
spume	skew	huge
bugle ★	view ★	humid
view ★	dispute ★	acute
curfew	preview ★	
dispute ★	argue	
preview ★	bugle ★	
music		
utensil		
amusement		
cucumber		
avenue		
perfume		

Versatile Varmints As you have discovered, some words can be used as different parts of speech. Use the following words in sentences that demonstrate how they can work as nouns (**n**) or verbs (**v**). Then, indicate if the word was used as a noun or a verb. Examples are provided to help you get started.

You can **rescue** the blue emu. (**v**) The **rescue** was successful. (**n**)

Example answers:

view	**n/v**
From the house, there was a breathtaking view of the dump.	n
I do not view life next to a dump as all that wonderful.	v

dispute	
The dispute was over who deserved to eat the last pickle.	n
I certainly did dispute the decision, since I deserved to eat that pickle.	v

cue	
I missed my cue and stumbled late onto the stage.	n
Ethyl tried to cue him in, but Bert wouldn't listen.	v

Word Detective A good dictionary will give amazing information about the history of words. Investigate the origins of some of this lesson's study words.

A Few Curfews

You would think that the words **few** and **curfew** would be related, but they're not! **Few** comes from an Anglo-Saxon word for "little." That makes sense, because if you have only a **few** chickens, then you may not have enough.

But where does the word **curfew** come from? What was its original meaning?

The word **curfew** comes from the French **covrefeu**, which meant "a signal to cover the hearth fire" (from the root **covrir**, meaning "to cover").

Bugling Bovines

The word **bugle** has something to do with cattle. See if you can find how **cattle** bungled into bugle.

The word **bugle** comes through the Anglo-Saxon word for a horn from a wild ox used for drinking or as a hunting horn. That word derived from the Latin **buculus** ("young ox") and **bos** ("head of cattle").

Whose Muse?

The words **music** and **amusement** both share the same root—**muse**. Amuse yourself by finding out what a **muse** is.

A **muse** is any of the nine sister goddesses in Greek mythology who preside over song, poetry, and the arts and sciences. Each muse is considered to be a specific source of inspiration among the disciplines in these areas.

Spelling Concept: Homophone Home Because you know that **homo** means "the same" and **phone** means "sound," you know that **homophones** are words that sound the same but are spelled differently and have different meanings.

Since there are several ways of representing the /yū/ sound in our spelling system, you knew there'd be homophones sharing this sound. Let's fiddle with a few.

Read through these sets of /yū/ homophones. Then, circle two of the sets. Use each set in a sentence that demonstrates the different meanings of the homophones.

you / ewe / yew   few / phew   cue / queue   hue / hew / Hugh

Answers will vary.

1. ______________________________

____

____

____

____

2. ______________________________

____

____

____

____

Spelling Concept: You now know that the spellings **u**, **ue**, **ew**, and **u(c)e** can represent both the /ū/ and /yū/ vowel sounds.

Dictation Get ready to write this paragraph to dictation.

Perfumed and dressed to the nines, Judy looked truly cute. She joined a few of her friends, who had found amusement at a kids' club down the avenue. While the music spewed from the jukebox, students danced until their curfew. Without arguing, they went home on cue in the humid Utah night.

Magic Squares Build words using the letters in each of these magic squares.

Magic Square

c	r	t
e	u(c)e	d
l	f	h

Magic Square

f	ch	p
l	ew	r
t	s	c

Magic Square

h	r	t
c	ue	f
b	l	g

Magic Square

t	j	c
l	u	d
b	FREE vowel	n

Speed Read Time yourself on three different days reading this list of words out loud (across from left to right). Keep track of your times and errors. Notice how words with similar spellings can have /yū/ or /ū/ vowel sounds.

humor rumor	fuel rule	fuse choose	cupid stupid
mute suit root	few dew	hue Sue	cube rube
cute shoot	emu Esu	fuel stool	hew chew
pupil ruble	fuse choose	cue rue	few new
you cue cute	bun pun puny	pew spew spume	
hum humid	hug huge	pup pupa pupil	hue cue rescue
rub ruby	fuss fuse	cub cube Cuban	
human humane	unit unite	bug bugle	cut cute
tub tuba	ton tune	stud student	plum plume
jut jute	dud dude	mutt mute	cup cupid

dispute repute
muse amuse amusement
refuse infuse defuse confuse
reduce produce reproduce

compute computer
view preview review interview
induce introduce

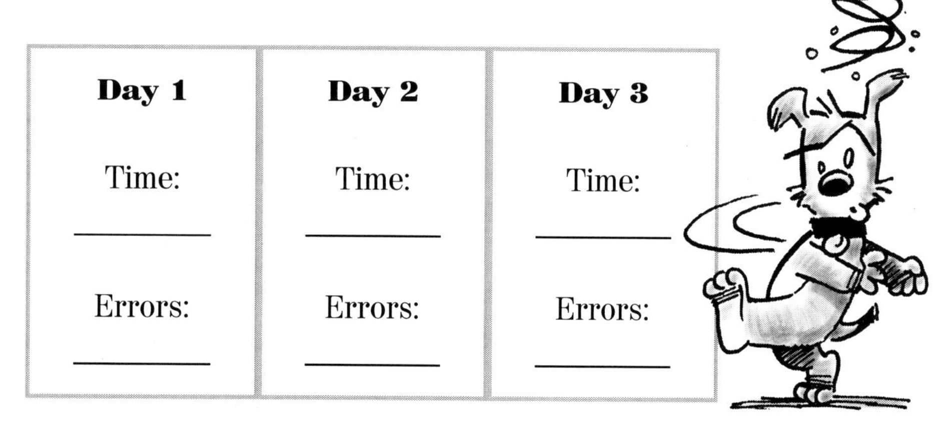

Day 1	Day 2	Day 3
Time: ________	Time: ________	Time: ________
Errors: ________	Errors: ________	Errors: ________

Finally: Take the Posttest, and record your score here. **Number Correct:** __________

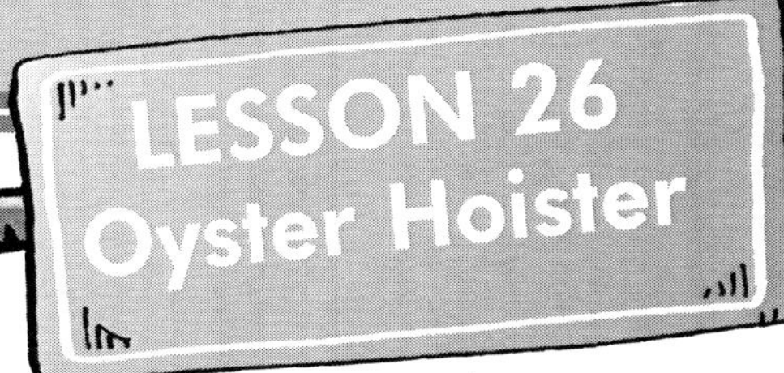

Phonemic Awareness Activities

1. **Segmentation Activity** Hold up the number of fingers—or show the number of markers—that is equal to the number of sounds (phonemes) in each of these words. (Count /oi/ as one sound.)

joy	**enjoy**	**coy**	**coil**	**coiled**	
/j/ /oi/	/ĕ/ /n/ /j/ /oi/	/k/ /oi/	/k/ /oi/ /l/	/k/ /oi/ /l/ /d/	
boy	**boil**	**boiled**	**boiler**	**cot**	**boycott**
/b/ /oi/	/b/ /oi/ /l/	/b/ /oi/ /l/ /d/	/b/ /oi/ /l/ /er/	/k/ /ŏ/ /t/	/b/ /oi/ /k/ /ŏ/ /t/
oil	**soil**	**spoil**	**spoiled**	**term**	**turmoil**
/oi/ /l/	/s/ /oi/ /l/	/s/ /p/ /oi/ /l/	/s/ p/ /oi/ /l/ /d/	/t/ /er/ /m/	/t/ /er/ /m/ /oi/ /l/
joy	**join**	**joint**	**point**	**pointed**	
/j/ /oi/	/j/ /oi/ /n/	/j/ /oi/ /n/ /t/	/p/ /oi/ /n/ /t/	/p/ /oi/ /n/ /t/ /ĭ/ /d/	
void	**avoid**	**avoided**	**foil**	**foiled**	
/v/ /oi/ /d/	/ŭ/ /v/ /oi/ /d/	/ŭ/ /v/ /oi/ /d/ /ĭ/ /d/	/f/ /oi/ /l/	/f/ /oi/ /l/ /d/	
Roy	**Troy**	**destroy**	**destroyed**		
/r/ /oi/	/t/ /r/ /oi/	/d/ /ĭ/ /s/ /t/ /r/ /oi/	/d/ /ĭ/ /s/ /t/ /r/ /oi/ /d/		
core	**cord**	**corduroy**	**voice**	**choice**	**moist**
/k/ /or/	/k/ /or/ /d/	/k/ /or/ /d/ /er/ /oi/	/v/ /oi/ /s/	/ch/ /oi/ /s/	/m/ /oi/ /s/ /t/

Phonemic Awareness Activities (Continued)

2. **Substitution Task** Substitute the first sound with the second sound to make a new word.

foist /f/ – /m/	**soil** /s/ – /t/	**coin** /k/ – /j/	**joy** /j/ – /b/
royal /r/ – /l/	**coil** /k/ – /f/	**choice** /ch/ – /v/	**moist** /m/ – /h/
boil /b/ – /s/	**choice** /oi/ – /ā/	**spoil** /oi/ – /ĕ/	**coil** /oi/ – /aw/
coin /oi/ – /ē/	**foist** /oi/ – /ă/	**boil** /oi/ – /ĭ/	**coin** /oi/ – /ā/

3. **Deletion Task** Say each word after deleting the identified sound (phoneme).

spoil without /p/	**coil** without /k/	**coin** without /n/	**joint** without /t/
Troy without /r/	**boink** without /b/	**boiler** without /er/	**spoiled** without /d/

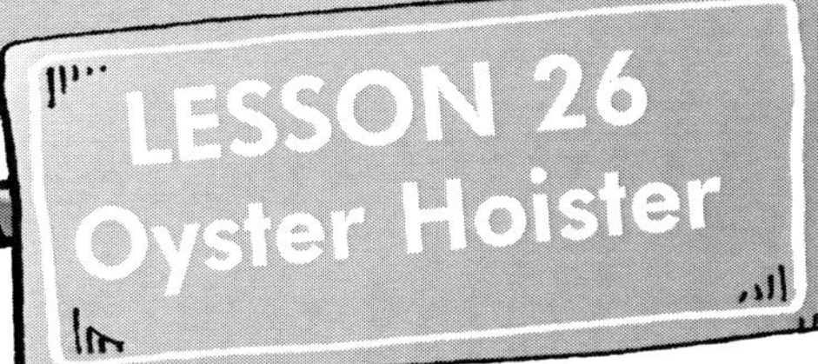

LESSON 26 Oyster Hoister

Dictate words in the lesson word list for Pretest and Posttest administration. Modify the number of words as needed.

Lesson 26 Word List

1. oil
2. joy
3. join
4. decoy
5. boiler
6. soybean
7. voice
8. royal
9. moist
10. destroy
11. noise
12. spoiled
13. choice
14. annoy
15. boyfriend
16. pointless
17. foisted
18. deploy
19. boycott
20. turmoil
21. employment
22. exploit
23. corduroy
24. joyfully

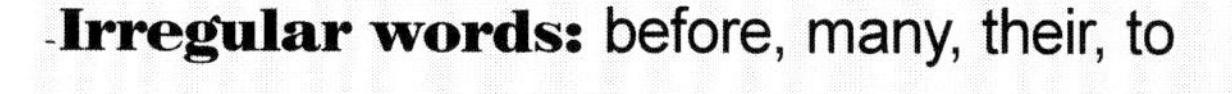

Irregular words: before, many, their, to

Spelling Concept: The **diphthong** /oi/ is spelled with <u>**oi**</u> (as in **boil**) or <u>**oy**</u> (as in **boy**).

All of this lesson's study words contain the /oi/ sound. Look at yourself in a mirror or watch a partner say "Enjoy the toy boy" five times fast. Now, try to say this without moving your lips!

You will notice how your lips start in a round position, then move out to a smile position (or a grimace position if you overdo it) to make the /oi/ sound. You might wonder why the /oi/ sound is considered one sound and not two sounds. Professor Fuzzy Thunker thinks about things like that. Do you want to be like him?

The important thing is that it isn't that hard to learn when to use <u>**oi**</u> and when to use <u>**oy**</u> to spell the /oi/ sound. The choice depends on the position in a word or a syllable where you hear /oi/. Let's check it out.

Underline the letter or letter patterns in this lesson's spelling words that represent the /oi/ sound. (Do not include the irregular words.) Then, sort the words into one of the two given groups.

Lesson 26 Word List

1. oil
2. joy
3. join
4. decoy
5. boiler
6. soybean
7. voice
8. royal
9. moist
10. destroy
11. noise
12. spoiled
13. choice
14. annoy
15. boyfriend
16. pointless
17. foisted
18. deploy
19. boycott
20. turmoil
21. employment
22. exploit
23. corduroy
24. joyfully

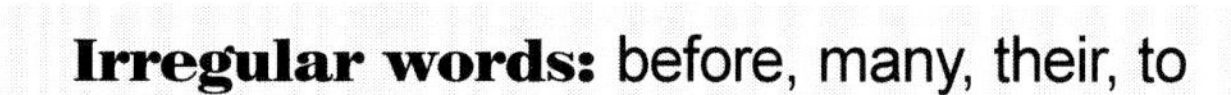

Irregular words: before, many, their, to

/oi/ = oi
(as in **oil**)

oil	foisted
join	turmoil
boiler	exploit
voice	foil ★
moist	point ★
noise	joint ★
spoiled	coil ★
choice	soil ★
pointless	poison ★

/oi/ = oy
(as in **boy**)

joy	employment
decoy	curduroy
soybean	joyfully
royal	voyage ★
destroy	loyal ★
annoy	royal ★
boyfriend	toy ★
deploy	enjoy ★
boycott	oyster ★

Example answers are starred (★).

Word Find Add two or more different words to each group above. Put a star (★) next to the words you add.

Alphabet Soup Write each set of words in alphabetical order.

a b c d e f g h i j k l m n o p q r s t u v w x y z

Set 1:

destroy employment decoy exploit deploy

1. decoy
2. deploy
3. destroy
4. employment
5. exploit

Set 2:

joy oil spoiled moist join soybean joyfully noise point royal

1. join
2. joy
3. joyfully
4. moist
5. noise
6. oil
7. point
8. royal
9. soybean
10. spoiled

Divide this lesson's study words into syllables. (Do not include the irregular words.) Then, underline all of the vowel team *syllables* that include the **oi** and **oy** spellings. Finally, list eight **oi** syllables and eight **oy** syllables.

Lesson 26 Word List

1. oil	9. moist	17. foist/ed
2. joy	10. de/stroy	18. de/ploy
3. join	11. noise	19. boy/cott
4. de/coy	12. spoiled	20. tur/moil
5. boil/er	13. choice	21. em/ploy/ment
6. soy/bean	14. an/noy	22. ex/ploit
7. voice	15. boy/friend	23. cor/du/roy
8. roy/al	16. point/less	24. joy/ful/ly

Irregular words: before, many, their, to

oi Syllables		**oy Syllables**	
oil	spoiled	joy	boy
join	choice	coy	ploy
boil	point	soy	
voice	foist	roy	
moist	moil	stroy	
noise	ploit	noy	

a. Where in a syllable or word do you find the **oi** spelling for /oi/?

The oi spelling for /oi/ is found when followed by one or more consonant sounds and spellings.

b. Where in a syllable or word do you find the **oy** spelling for /oi/?

The oy spelling for /oi/ is found in the final, or end, position of a syllable or a word.

Build as many words as you can by combining the given letters and letter groups.

c b f m s j t l h sp br sirl

oin	**oil**	**oist**
coin	coil	foist
loin	foil	hoist
join	spoil	moist
sirloin	boil	joist
	soil	
	toil	
	broil	

Now that you know about <u>oi</u> and <u>oy</u>, you can rejoice! You will no longer be foiled by your inner turmoil over this choice (nor be called maladroit). Now, employ your new knowledge by filling in the blanks with **<u>oi</u>** or **<u>oy</u>** to complete each word.

_oi_l	b_oy_	enj_oy_	j_oi_n
v_oi_d	t_oy_	dec_oy_	p_oi_nt
ann_oy_	m_oi_st	s_oy_bean	f_ow_l
h_oi_st	b_oy_cott	n_oi_se	destr_oy_
turm_oi_l	dev_oi_d	l_oy_al	empl_oy_
v_oi_ce	b_oy_friend	depl_oy_	f_oi_st
av_oi_d	expl_oi_t	cordur_oy_	embr_oi_der

a. How many of these words can you use in one *meaningful* sentence?

____

____

____

____

____

Answers will vary.

OK, wise guy/gal; tell what a **compound** word is. Then, build a few with each of these words.

A compound word is formed when two smaller words—which can each stand alone as independent words—are combined, hyphenated, or separated. These words often add their combined meaning to the meaning of the compound (as in **sailboat**), but not always (as in **oilskin**). The compounding form of word-building is an Anglo-Saxon pattern.

Example answers:

oil	**boy**
oilcan	boyfriend
oilcloth	boyhood
oil painting	Boy Scout
oil pan	bellboy
oil field	batboy
oil slick	tomboy
oil well	boycott

Word Detective A good dictionary will give amazing information about the history of words. Investigate the origins of some of this week's study words.

a. Even ancient humans with names like Grum and Ugwort used oil. There are many kinds of oil, including the oil the Tin Man used after getting caught in the rain. Where does the word **oil** come from? What is the basic definition of oil?

The word **oil** comes from the Greek word for "olive." How many of you and your parents use olive oil in cooking or on bread instead of butter? It's delicious! The basic definition of **oil** is "various greasy and combustible substances coming from animal, vegetable, and mineral sources."

b. Brainstorm a spiderweb map showing all the things you can think of that have some connection to oil (maybe even a boyfriend or a goilfriend).

Example answers:

Motor Oil
cars
motorcycles
lawnmowers

Body Oil
hand cream
hair gel
massage oil

Oil and the Environment
oil spills
Alaskan wildlife
global warming

Edible Oil
canola
peanut
olive
sesame

Oil Production
refineries
tankers
oil wells
oil platforms

Oil Politics
OPEC
Middle East
alternative energy sources

Exercise 8 (Continued)

c. You might think that the words **boycott** and **boychick** are compound words, but they're NOT! Use your word-detective skills to find out where these two words come from and what they mean.

boycott: "to refuse to have anything to do with something"

This word was coined in 1877 after its namesake, Charles C. Boycott.

A British land agent in Ireland, Boycott was socially excluded because of his

refusal to reduce rents on properties.

boychick: "a young man or boy"

This word comes from American Yiddish by combining the root **boy** with the

Yiddish suffix **-tshik** ("small"). It does make sense, however, as a compound

because the **chick** part has a similar meaning to the Yiddish suffix.

d. The word **foist** comes from the Anglo-Saxon word **fyst**, meaning "fist." What does **foist** have to do with a fist?

The word **foist** means "to take into one's own hands by forcing something on

another."

Parting Your Speech Find at least four words in this lesson's word list for each of these parts of speech. (Do not include the irregular words.) Star (★) those words that can function as more than one part of speech. You will not use all the words.

Lesson 26 Word List

1. oil	7. voice	13. choice	19. boycott
2. joy	8. royal	14. annoy	20. turmoil
3. join	9. moist	15. boyfriend	21. employment
4. decoy	10. destroy	16. pointless	22. exploit
5. boiler	11. noise	17. foisted	23. corduroy
6. soybean	12. spoiled	18. deploy	24. joyfully

Irregular words: before, many, their, to

Nouns	Verbs	Adjectives
oil ★	oil ★	royal
joy	join	moist
decoy ★	decoy ★	spoiled ★
boiler	destroy	choice ★
soybean	voice ★	pointless
voice ★	spoiled ★	corduroy ★
noise	annoy	
choice ★	foisted	
boyfriend	deploy	
boycott ★	boycott ★	
turmoil	exploit ★	
employment		
corduroy ★		
exploit ★		

Versatile Varmints Use these words in sentences that demonstrate their duty as nouns, verbs, or adjectives.

oil

The oil made Clem rich, so he moved to Beverly Hills. (n)

Maybe we should oil your head so it doesn't rust. (v)

point

The point is that children are funnier-looking these days. (n)

If you point your finger at me again, I'll dip it in salad dressing. (v)

boil (the noun form of **boil** is pretty gross)

The boil that erupted on Herman's nose was bright red. (n)

Be sure to boil the water for seven minutes before you drink it, or you might end up like Herman. (v)

choice

The choice is clear: you can be part of the problem or part of the solution. (n) We carry nothing but the most choice doggie-care products in our shop. (adj.)

Sentence Dictations Study these sentences until you can write them fluently and flawlessly.

1. Food made with soybean oil can spoil in moist, humid weather.

2. The migrant grape pickers felt exploited and went on strike. Many lost their employment when the boycott of grapes threw the fruit industry into turmoil.

3. Joy was annoyed with her boyfriend because he foisted his decision on her before offering her a choice.

4. Please use a quiet voice to reduce the noise.

Exercise 12

Exercise #12: Speed Read Time yourself on three different occasions reading out loud Thunker's infamous account of the demise of the oyster hoister, Roy Doyle.

Roy Doyle, Oyster Hoister

Roy Doyle was an oyster hoister employed by the Royal Oyster and Cracker Crumb Company. In his oilcloth slicker and soiled boots, Doyle toiled in the moist mud flats of Troy. There, he foisted himself upon countless oysters that he annoyed and destroyed as he hoisted them from their warm and oozy beds. Doyle enjoyed hoisting oysters from the moist mud of Troy until one day the annoyed oysters came up with a ploy. They foiled Doyle by spewing poisonous oyster ointment at his loins, causing Doyle's skin to boil and Doyle to recoil. This ploy diminished Doyle's enjoyment of oyster hoisting and left Doyle with no choice but to avoid oysters and find other employment. Doyle's demise had a flamboyant—though not buoyant—ending when his steamer sank on the voyage home to Boise.

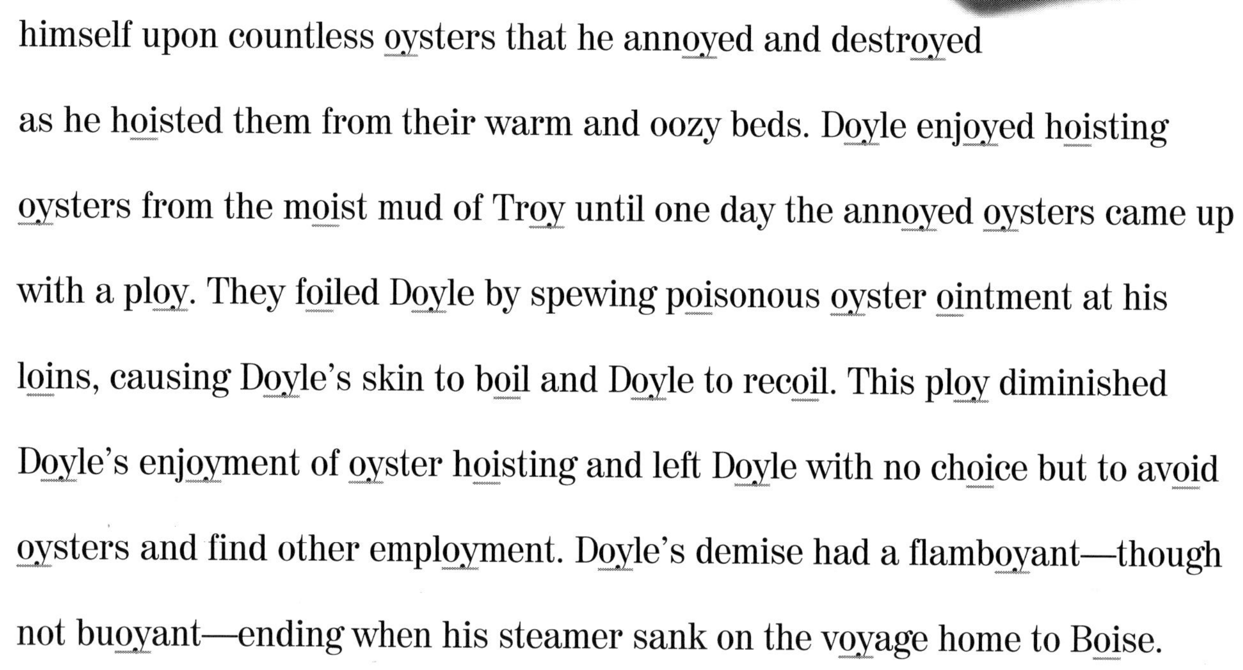

Day 1	Day 2	Day 3
Time: ________	Time: ________	Time: ________
Errors: ________	Errors: ________	Errors: ________

Challenge Activity

1. How many /oi/ spellings are there in Roy's story? 56

Finally: Take the Posttest, and record your score here. **Number Correct:** __________

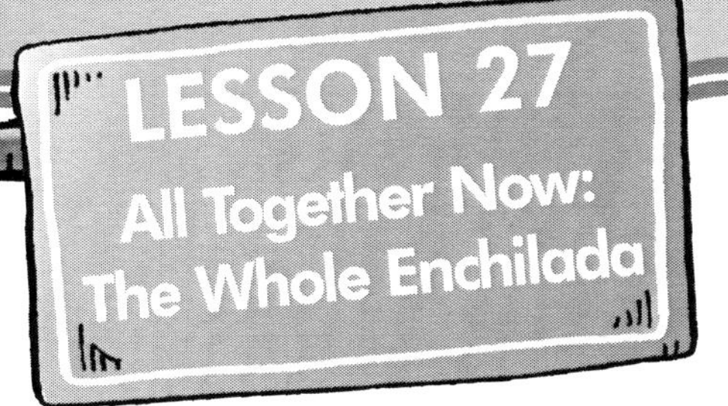

Congratulations! You've made it through 26 thrilling and mind-numbing spelling lessons to reach this point (or you're confused and you've opened this book backwards). Now is a good time to step back and see how far you've come. This lesson will be a walk down memory lane (unless you don't remember anything!). So let's revisit the biggest hits of *Spellography: A Student Road Map to Better Spelling*.

Spelling Concept #1: There are two classes of speech sounds: **consonant dogs** and **vowel cats**.

Individual speech sounds are called **phonemes**. **Vowel phonemes** are different from **consonant phonemes**. For one thing, there are fewer vowel sounds than consonant sounds, so vowel sounds think that they are special . . . like cats. We make vowel sounds without blocking the airstream from our mouths (like caterwauling cats). For this reason, we call vowel sounds **open sounds**.

We block the flow of air when we make **consonant sounds**. We use our teeth, our lips, our tongues, and our noses to block or obstruct the vocal airflow from our chests and lungs out of our mouths (like growling dogs). Because of this air-blocking, we call **consonant sounds** closed sounds. Some consonant sounds are more closed than others, and leaky consonant sounds can seem vowel-like. This leaky consonant club includes the /w/, /y/, /r/, /l/, /n/, /m/, and /ng/ sounds. Because these leaky consonant sounds aren't completely closed, they can alter neighboring sounds and cause confusion. Students and teachers often dread these leaky sounds.

Sing the following lyrics from "Oh, Susanna." Then, sing them again, but this time hold each word. Write down the *sound* you hold longest for each word.

It	rained	all	night	the	day	I	left
/ĭ/	/ā/	/aw/	/ī/	/ŭ/	/ā/	/ī/	/ĕ/

The	weather	it	was	dry
/ŭ/	/ĕ/ /er/	/ĭ/	/ŭ/	/ī/

a. (When you think about it, "Oh, Susanna" is a pretty weird song!) Anyway, sort the longest-held sounds into vowel sounds and consonant sounds (phonemes).

Vowel phonemes	Consonant phonemes
/ĭ/, /ā/, /aw/, /ī/, /ŭ/, /ĕ/, /er/	(none)

b. Are there more vowel cats or more consonant dogs? Why do you think this is so?

There are more vowel cats. Vowel sounds are open sounds, made without blocking vocal air. When we sing, it's easy and natural to hold vowel sounds. On the other hand, vocal air is partly or totally blocked when we make consonant dog sounds; so, we have less air to hold consonant sounds when we sing.

Spelling Concept #2: We have only 26 letters in the English alphabet to represent 40+ speech sounds; accomplishing this feat requires some trickery. Among the tricks are (1) single letters that represent more than one speech sound; and (2) groups of letters that combine to represent one, sometimes new, sound.

Underline the letters c, g, x, and y in these words. Then, sort the words into the given pronunciation categories. Some words will apply to more than one category; star (★) those words. Finally, add two new words to each group and then answer the questions that follow.

mice	pencil	city	
germ	yoga	myth	
hype	guess	toxic	
index	cord	next	
extra	plug	stage	gorge
exam	center	cube	dynamic
crab	comb	symbol	gumbo
bypass	gyro	suffix	hydrogen
giant	yucky	youth	wax
exist	cyclone	glass	gypsy
tragic	exempt	yellow	text
cattle	fancy	funny	

Words with c

Hard /k/ (as in **cat**)	Soft /s/ (as in **cent**)
tragic ★	mice
cube	pencil
cord	cyclone ★
toxic ★	city ★
cattle	fancy ★
crab	center
comb	***fence***
cyclone ★	***niece***
dynamic ★	
yucky ★	
camera	
crib	

Words with g

Hard /g/ (as in **get**)	Soft /j/ (as in **gem**)
glass	gyro ★
plug	hydrogen ★
gorge ★	stage
gumbo	germ
guess	gypsy ★
yoga ★	tragic ★
bug	giant
grain	gorge ★
	ginger
	strange

Words with x

/ks/ (as in **box**)	Soft /gz/ (as in **exit**)
wax	exist
toxic ★	exam
extra	exempt
index	***exhaust***
suffix	***executive***
text	
next	
axle	
explain	

Examples of new words are in *bold italic.*

Exercise 2 (Continued)

mice	**giant**	**plug**	**city**	**youth**	**wax**
germ	**exist**	**center**	**myth**	**glass**	**gypsy**
hype	**tragic**	**comb**	**toxic**	**yellow**	**text**
index	**cattle**	**gyro**	**next**	**funny**	
extra	**pencil**	**yucky**	**stage**	**gorge**	
exam	**yoga**	**cyclone**	**cube**	**dynamic**	
crab	**guess**	**exempt**	**symbol**	**gumbo**	
bypass	**cord**	**fancy**	**suffix**	**hydrogen**	

Words with y

/y/ (as in **y**ell)	/ĭ/ (as in g**y**m)	/ī/ (as in cr**y**)	/ē/ (as in bab**y**)
yellow	gypsy ★	gyro ★	city ★
youth	myth	hydrogen ★	fancy ★
yucky ★	symbol	hype	yucky ★
yoga ★	***typical***	cyclone ★	gypsy ★
young	***cymbal***	dynamic ★	funny
yak	***lynx***	bypass	***lazy***
		type	***dirty***
		dynamite	

Examples of new words are in ***bold italic***.

1. What pattern shows you that **c** sounds like /k/?

   The letter **c** is pronounced /k/ when followed by the vowels **a** (**cat**), **o** (**cot**), or **u** (**cut**); or when followed by any consonant (**clam**, **cram**); or in the final position of a word (**plastic**).

   What pattern shows you that **c** sounds like /s/?

   The letter **c** is pronounced /s/ when followed by the vowels **e** (**cent**), **i** (**city**), or **y** (**cycle**).

2. What pattern shows you that **g** sounds like /j/?

The letter g is pronounced as a soft /j/ when it is followed by the vowels e (**gent**), i (**gin**), and y (**gym**). (There are a few exceptions to the soft g pattern, such as **gear** or **gimp**.)

What pattern shows you that **g** sounds like /g/?

The letter g is pronounced hard /g/ when it is followed by the vowels a (**gal**), o (**got**), and u (**gum**), or when it is followed by any consonant (**ghastly**, **glad**, **grab**) except n. In the combination gn, the g is silent and the n is pronounced (**gnaw**, **gnat**; **benign**, **campaign**).

3. What pattern shows you when y represents:

a. The consonant /y/ (**yellow**) sound?

When y is found in the initial (beginning) position of a word or syllable.

b. The short /ĭ/ (**gym**) sound?

When the y is found in a closed syllable. This y spelling pattern is found mostly in words of Greek origin (**gymnasium**, **gyroscope**).

c. The long /ī/ (**by**) or long /ē/ (**baby**)?

When the y is found in the final (end) position of a word or syllable. The letter y can be used as an ending to make an adjective (**noisy**, **sloppy**), or as part of the suffix -ly, to make an adverb (**noisily**, **sloppily**).

Spelling Concept #3: The position in a word (beginning, middle, or end) in which we hear a sound—as well as the neighboring sounds—gives us clues for spelling.

Early on, we studied how the /k/ sound can be spelled many different ways. We find the /k/ sound included in consonant blends and in weird places—like in <u>x</u>. Give the *position* in a word in which you are likely to find the following spellings that include this /k/ sound. Then, give two example words for each spelling pattern.

	Position	Example Words
1. The letter <u>c</u> represents /k/	a. at the end of a word	plastic, magic
	b. before vowels a, o, u	cat, cot, cut
	c. before a consonant	clam, exact
2. The letters <u>ck</u> represent /k/	a. after a short vowel	pickle, tacky
	b. in a one-syllable word	pack, trick
3. The letter <u>k</u> alone represents /k/	a. before vowels e, i, y	keep, kit, kyack
	b. in the final position after a consonant	risk, tank
4. The letters <u>qu</u> represent /kw/	a. in the initial position	queen, quick
	b. in the middle of a word or a syllable	square, require
5. The letter <u>x</u> represents /ks/	a. often at the end of a word or a syllable	box, next, extra, lexicon

Exercise 3b

Fill in the blanks with one of the five spelling patterns that include the /k/ sound listed in Exercise #3a. Remember to think about the position clues!

s_c_an	sna_ck_	tas_k_	a_x_	_k_eg
_c_ube	sta_ck_	s_k_id (squid)	_qu_iz	fi_x_
_k_eep	stu_ck_	_c_raft	wa_x_	clo_ck_
smo_k_e	_qu_ilt	o_x_	_k_ilt (quilt)	bla_ck_
s_qu_irm	ne_x_t	_k_ing	bra_k_e	s_c_ar
_qu_estion	sunde_ck_	s_k_in	inde_x_	shrin_k_
_c_lash	Yan_k_ee	be_c_ome	s_qu_int	stri_k_e
_c_u_c_umber	par_k_	s_c_orch	comple_x_	_c_ampus
_k_iss	_c_urfew	_k_i_ck_ (quick)	tri_ck_	_k_ya_ck_
don_k_ey	_c_omet	fla_k_e	s_qu_irrel	_c_ran_k_

Construct a *meaningful* sentence that includes as many /k/ sounds as you can. Circle all of the spellings that represent the /k/ sound in your sentence. Read your sentence to your classmates. Can they identify the number of /k/ sounds you used? **Example answer:**

King Max clashed with the quick, slick, crafty Clem the Clod because Clem's ax struck the skin of the king's ox, causing a scar on its black back.

Challenge Activity How many words that either begin or end with the /k/ sound can you write *in a row* in a sentence? **Answers will vary.**

___

___

___

Spelling Concept #4: We use letter combinations to represent sounds that are often different from any of the individual sounds the letters represent on their own. This way, we can represent more than 26 sounds with just 26 letters. We call these letter combinations that represent one sound **di** (two-letter) and **tri** (three-letter) **graphs**.

Underline the **digraphs** and **trigraphs** in these words. Then, add six more words that contain digraphs or trigraphs.

ditch	shack	whip	bash	then	shush
check	budge	thank	wham	scratch	smudge

Example answers:

thatch	thank	fudge
charm	shadow	whip

Spelling Concept #5: The patterns for using the endings **-ch/-tch**, **-ge/-dge**, and **-k/-ck** are similar.

1. After a strong, long vowel or a sounded consonant, use:
   -ch (co**a**ch, bu**n**ch)
   -ge (p**a**ge, ra**n**ge)
   k (b**ea**k, ba**n**k, ba**r**k)

2. Weak, short vowels need extra support, so add the extra letter and use:
   -tch (m**a**tch)
   -dge (b**a**dge)
   -ck (b**a**ck)

These blanks need to be filled in with either the /ch/, /j/, or /k/ sound to complete each word. Where there is a single vowel, try using the short vowel sound along with these consonant sounds to form a word. Make each word different.

ba_tch_ ba_dge_ ba_ck_ coa_ch_ co_k_e mas_k_

bea_ch_ bea_k_ hin_ge_ pa_tch_ pa_ge_ pa_ck_

gru_dge_ skun_k_ hu_ge_ (hutch) ben_ch_ char_ge_ bul_k_ (bulge)

cree_k_ ca_ge_ (catch) sta_ge_ sta_ck_ bran_ch_ pea_ch_

shar_k_ sna_tch_ sna_ck_ oa_k_ we_dge_ tor_ch_

Thunkering About It You are now the master of complex consonant spellings . . . or you are now not a disaster at complex consonant spellings . . . or you are getting a complex about complex consonant spellings. Whatever! Here's a chance to prove your mettle (or your muddle). Repair this stinky entry from Thunker's journal before it disturbs you.

I ~~kamped~~ camped out on the ~~dec~~ deck of my ~~bric~~ brick ~~portch~~ porch to ~~wach~~ watch for ~~skunes~~ skunks. ~~There~~ Their ~~lodg~~ lodge is ~~neckst~~ next to the ~~beetch~~ beech tree out ~~bac~~ back. We ~~learnd~~ learned this ~~wen~~ when Bess ~~spoockt~~ spooked a ~~lardge~~ large ~~scunk~~ skunk while ~~feching~~ fetching a ~~stic~~ stick. This ~~shockt~~ shocked skunk ~~skwirtid~~ squirted a ~~bach~~ batch of musty ~~sluge~~ sludge, ~~witch~~ which ~~drentched~~ drenched Bess's belly, snout, and all. Now, Bess ~~stincks~~ stinks ~~lick~~ like a ~~skwid~~ squid, ~~witch~~ which I find disturbing!

Challenge Activity How many misspelled or misused words did you find and correct? _28_

Spelling Concept #6: There are 18 vowel sounds in English, including the three vowel + -r (v + -r) sounds and two diphthong vowel sounds in our Vowel Sounds Chart (Lesson 11—Valley of the Vowels). We can organize or group these vowel sounds by the formations we make with our mouths as we say them.

This group of words includes vowel sounds made in the front of our mouths in a "smiley" position. As you make these **front vowel** sounds, your tongue gradually drops, pushing down your jaw. Sort these words—in order from highest to lowest jaw position—into these six groups. Then, add two new words to each group.

fish	tub	fetch
bed	mat	spray
pluck	heat	theme
feet	rain	batch
nap	web	trick
fix	jump	stake

/ē/ (as in **eat**)	/ĭ/ (as in **itch**)	/ā/ (as in **ate**)	/ĕ/ (as in **Ed**)	/ă/ (as in **apple**)	/ŭ/ (as in **up**)
heat	fish	spray	fetch	mat	tub
theme	trick	rain	bed	batch	jump
feet	fix	stake	web	nap	pluck
treat ★	sit ★	bake ★	sled ★	track ★	gut ★
three ★	slid ★	came ★	neck ★	slab ★	flood ★

Example answers are starred (★).

This group of words includes the two vowel sounds made when your mouth is most open, with your lower jaw in its lowest position. Sort these **low**, **open vowel** words into these two groups, and add at least two new words to each group.

pop	cause
law	frog
haul	chop
plod	vault
crawl	botch
block	squawk

/ŏ/ (as in **odd**)		/aw/ (as in **saw**)	
pop	spot ★	cause	law
plod	drop ★	haul	squawk
block	blob ★	vault	fault ★
chop	notch ★	crawl	jaw ★
botch	stock ★	frog	dawdle ★

Example answers are starred (★).

This group of words includes vowel sounds that are made in the back of your mouth, with your lips moving to a round position. Sort these **round vowel** words into these three groups, and add two new words to each group.

book	flute	zoo	glue	blow	flown
stew	nose	good	stood	broom	proof
soak	crook	roach	quote	soup	tune

/ō/ (as in **oat**)	/ŏo/ (as in **foot**)	/ū/ (as in **boot**)
blow	book	zoo
soak	good	broom
roach	stood	soup
flown	crook	flute
nose	shook ★	stew
quote	wood ★	glue
glow ★	hood ★	proof
doze ★	could ★	tune
toast ★	hook ★	truth ★
hobo ★	should ★	tooth ★
		tulip ★
		prune ★

Example answers are starred (★).

This group of words has vowel sounds that are changed by the vowel-like /r/ sound that is glued to the vowel. Sort these vowel + **-r** (**v + -r**) words into the given groups, and add at least two new words to each group.

fern	tar	shark	north	scarf	horse
fork	burn	swirl	perch	burst	birch

/er/ (as in **her**, **sir**, **fur**)	/or/ (as in **corn**)	/ar/ (as in **far**)
fern	north	tar
perch	fork	scarf
burn	horse	shark
burst	sport ★	yard ★
swirl	porch ★	card ★
birch	storm ★	bark ★
jerk ★	forge ★	arch ★
firm ★	scorch ★	harp ★

Example answers are starred (★).

This group of words has **diphthong vowel** sounds that are made by moving your mouth from one position to another (/oi/ and /ou/), the long /ī/ vowel (which is sometimes grouped with diphthongs), and the /yū/ combination. These vowel sounds seem as if they are two sounds in one. Sort these words among the four groups, and add at least two new words to each group.

pie	joy	cue	cute	fly	trout
spout	town	plow	bite	spew	fuse
few	why	moist	toy	choice	tribe

/ī/ (as in **try**)	/yū/ (as in **use**)	/ou/ (as in **cow**, **out**)	/oi/ (as in **boy**, **oil**)
pie	cue	spout	moist
bite	few	plow	joy
why	cute	town	toy
fly	spew	trout	choice
tribe	fuse	owl ★	coil ★
dine ★	huge ★	couch ★	foil ★
pine ★	hewn ★	louse ★	poise ★

Example answers are starred (★).

Spelling Concept #7: Each syllable has **one** vowel sound. There are six kinds of syllables that are used to include different vowel sounds: **closed**, **open**, **v + -r**, **vowel team**, **c + -le**, and **vc + -e** syllables. Knowledge of syllable types helps to identify how vowels sound when they are read and to make wise choices in spelling.

Sort these words by syllable type. Assign a syllable name to each column and put the words in the appropriate column. (There are a few two-syllable words that will apply to two different syllable groups according to their first and second syllables. Star [★] those words.)

ice	girl	tree	turtle	go	bunch	porch	berth
load	maple	rib	gray	cape	pry	no	eke
cat	he	rode	smart	glow	bugle	stream	marble

Closed **Syllable**	Open **Syllable**	v + -r **Syllable**	Vowel team **Syllable**	c + -le **Syllable**	vc + -e **Syllable**
rib	go	porch	tree	turtle ★	ice
cat	no	girl	load	maple ★	cape
bunch	glow	berth	stream	bugle ★	rode
	maple ★	smart	gray	marble ★	eke
	pry	turtle ★			
	he	marble ★			
	bugle ★				

Spelling Concept #8: We use **open**, **vc + -e**, and **vowel team** syllables to spell *long vowel sounds*; **closed** syllables to spell *short vowel sounds*; **v + -r** syllables to spell *vowel + -r sounds*; and **c + -le** syllables to spell a *common, final, unaccented syllable*.

Join the syllables in each group to form complete words.

smug	ple	smuggle	ath	pute	athlete
sta	tle	stable	dis	eze	dispute
dim	gle	dimple	cas	plode	cascade
ri	ble	rifle	trap	lete	trapeze
ti	fle	title	ex	cade	explode

bom	bit	bombard	boy	cet	boycott
mar	mish	market	tab	cer	tabloid
har	bard	harpoon	ex	cott	exploit
or	tress	orbit	sau	loid	saucer
for	cle	fortress	fau	ky	faucet
skir	poon	skirmish	gaw	ploit	gawky
cir	ket	circle			

re	cuss	reuse	row	dow	rowdy
un	plain	unless	coun	dy	county
dis	use	discuss	crow	ty	crowbar
sub	se	submit	yel	der	yellow
ex	mit	explain (expose)	win	low	window
com	less	compose (complain)	pow	bar	powder

Show the syllable breaks in these words. Then, label each syllable type accordingly:

o	=	open	**v + -r**	=	vowel + **-r**
c	=	closed	**vc + -e**	=	vowel, consonant + silent **-e**
vt	=	vowel team	**c + -le**	=	consonant + **-le**

daz/zle	wish/bone	splen/did	tur/moil
c c + -le	c vc + -e	c c	v + -r vt
cab/in	cra/dle	li/lac	lim/it
c c	o c + -le	o c	c c
fee/ble	thir/teen	dis/lo/cate	un/bro/ken
vt c + -le	v + -r vt	c o vc + -e	c o c

Spelling Concept #9: The **Anglo-Saxon** connection (good Old English)

Most of the words you have studied come to us from Anglo-Saxon, the foundation layer—the oldest form—of the English language. Evidence of Anglo-Saxon ancestry in modern English includes:

- The six syllable types we just reviewed
- The 100 most common words we use
- Consonant digraphs/trigraphs
- Consonant blends
- Vowel teams and diphthongs (/oi/, /ou/)
- **v + -r** combinations

In fact, most of the sound-to-letter matches in contemporary English—the way we sound out words—come from Anglo-Saxon, with only a few exceptions (like the way we use **y** for /i/ in **gym**, or **ph** for /f/ in **phone**). The letter **k** is used almost entirely in Anglo-Saxon words.

Sort the following Anglo-Saxon–based words among the given categories. Star (★) those words that apply to more than one category.

love	heart	knee	bird	fear	down	head	out
up	pickle	over	king	knight	horse	scold	sad
sheep	swim	cook	speak	dream	under	buckle	teacher
farmer	door	barrow	elbow	latch	lonesome	goat	chicken

Feelings	Animals	Body Parts	Common Things
love ★	sheep	knee ★	buckle ★
fear ★	goat	heart	latch ★
sad	bird	elbow ★	pickle ★
lonesome	horse	head	barrow
chicken ★	chicken ★		door

Common Verbs		Occupations	Direction Words
love ★	cook ★	knight	up
fear ★	buckle ★	cook ★	over
scold	pickle ★	farmer	down
dream	knee ★	king	out
swim	elbow ★	teacher	under
speak	latch ★		

Spelling Concept #10: One way of building longer words that is unique to the Anglo-Saxon heritage is to combine simple words (like **suit + case**) to form **compound** words (**suitcase**).

Use these words to build as many compound words as you can. You've got ten minutes. (Remember—compound words can be connected, hyphenated, or spaced apart.)

Example answers:

head (as in **headline**)	**down** (as in **down-home**)	**black** (as in **black hole**)
headache	downbeat	black-and-blue
headpiece	downcast	black-and-white
head cold	downfall	blackmail
headlight	down-to-earth	black belt
head start	downhill	blackberry
headdress	downgrade	blackjack
headstone	down under	black box
head off	downpour	black eye
headphone	downshift	black out
head-on	downsize	blackout

Spelling Concept #11: Another method of word-building is adding prefixes and suffixes to roots or base words. There are some familiar prefixes (**be-**, **for-**, **in-**, **mis-**, **out-**) and suffixes (**-ed**, **-ness**, **-ly**, **-ing**) that we use to build new forms of Anglo-Saxon–based roots.

Build as many words as you can in ten minutes by combining the roots or base words with the given prefixes and suffixes.

Prefixes

un- **mis-** **under-** **be-**

in- **out-** **over-**

Suffixes

-ly **-ing** **-ed** **-ness**

-er **-est** **-en**

Roots/Base Words

Example answers:

take	come	hard	true
untaken	become	hardly	untrue
mistaken	income	harder	trueness
undertake	overcome	harden	truest
outtake	coming	hardness	truly
taking	comer	hardest	truer
mistake	becoming	hardening	
mistakenly	outcome		
undertaking	overcoming		
overtake	unbecoming		
taken			

Concept #12: Homophones are words that sound the same but have different spellings and different meanings. It is easy to confuse—or be confused by—the similarities of homophones.

Thunker has had some scary experiences with homophones. Please fix the misguided words before they misguide you.

Thunker ~~herd~~ heard a noise like a ~~grown~~ groan coming from ~~hi~~ high above ~~hymn~~ him. He ~~guest~~ guessed that it was coming from the ~~beach~~ beech tree ~~buy~~ by his ~~feat~~ feet. Thunker ~~staired~~ stared upward ~~wear~~ where he saw something with black ~~fir~~ fur.

"It's a ~~bare~~ bear up ~~their~~ there!" Thunker ~~balled~~ bawled.

Now, Thunker had never ~~scene~~ seen a ~~bare~~ bear ~~be four~~ before, and he didn't ~~no~~ know what ~~two~~ to ~~dew~~ do. In his panic, Thunker tried ~~too flea~~ to flee, ~~butt~~ but he tripped over a tree ~~rute~~ root. Thunker landed on his ~~knows~~ nose, ~~witch~~ which caused him ~~grate pane~~ great pain. Just ~~than~~ then, Thunker ~~herd allowed creek~~ heard a loud creak followed by a ~~grate~~ great crack. He looked up to ~~sea~~ see a ~~tale~~ tail heading ~~rite four hymn~~ right for him. It landed like a ~~bolder write~~ boulder right on Thunker, along with a set of ~~pause~~ paws and ~~clause~~ claws and the ~~wrest~~ rest of its bulky self. ~~They're~~ There was quite a ~~seen~~ scene when Thunker rose to find Bess ~~rapped~~ wrapped around him like a ~~cheep~~ cheap shirt. Thunker was ~~soar~~ sore for ~~weaks~~ weeks after that, and he remained in a ~~fowl~~ foul mood—~~witch~~ which served him ~~write~~ right for being such a chicken.

Challenge Activity
How many homophone spelling errors did you find and correct? 52

Speed Read This is the last time—OK, the last three times—you will be asked to suffer through reading a Thunker clunker out loud. (Record your times and errors after each reading.) He hopes it leaves a lasting impression on you—three times over!

Last Licks

Thunker and Bess heard rowdies go
squeaking and whopping, squawking and screeching
through the fields and meadow below.

"Fleas and roaches! What encroaches?" wondered Thunker.

Into view did spew a rowdy crew,
led by Stupor Stu and others Thunker knew.

"Mumble, grumble!" grumbled Thunker.
"Why is that hodgepodge marching to my bunker?"

"We're here," replied the aged Sage Page,
"because your students have reached this stage."

"Each of them did what it took
to be ousted from this spelling book."

At that, Chunky Chucky struck a gong
and started chanting enchanted ranting
(which sounded to Thunker like chickens panting).

The singing vowel cats joined the jam,
along with Clem the fisherman.

The nose vowels hummed, the **-r** vowels rumbled,
Strange Georgia shook her rump and stumbled.

Urrg and Cora, Chip, Thor, and Mack
jittered up and down with Cracker Jack.

The Royal Oyster and Cracker Crumb Company sent oyster stew,
and the Moody Moose added special pickle and prune goo
(which he purchased while moaning about Sue in Peru).

While a rooster and an emu were heard to argue
over which was better, the stew or the goo.

And everyone made such a hullabaloo,
because they all were—and are—so proud of you!

Day 1	**Day 2**	**Day 3**
Time: ______	Time: ______	Time: ______
Errors: ______	Errors: ______	Errors: ______

YIPPEE!!

You have come to the end of a 27-lesson, spellographic tour of the English language. Don't you feel delirious?!

You are now a **truly** wise gal/guy. You have learned that the English language is not a scrambled, murky mess (like your bedroom or Thunker's hair). You have learned that there is order and logic to how English words are spelled and how new word forms are built. Take a moment to pat yourself on the back (or slap yourself in the head) for working so hard (hardly) to get to this point.

In the immortal words of Professor Fuzzy Thunker:

> "May *Webster* be with you always."

DICTIONARY